Story by Jun Lennon • Art by Maki Murakami

GRAVITATION
the novel

HAMBURG // LONDON // LOS ANGELES // TOKYO

Gravitation: The Novel
Story by Jun Lennon
Art by Maki Murakami

Translation - Andrew Cunningham
English Adaptation - Shahan Nerses
Copy Editors - Eric Althoff and Hope Donovan
Design and Layout - Jason Milligan
Cover Design - Seth Cable
Editor - Kara Stambach

Supervising Editor - Nicole Monastirsky
Digital Imaging Manager - Chris Buford
Production Managers - Jennifer Miller and Mutsumi Miyazaki
Managing Editor - Lindsey Johnston
VP of Production - Ron Klamert
Publisher and E.I.C. - Mike Kiley
President and C.O.O. - John Parker
C.E.O. - Stuart Levy

Special Thanks to Anna Sartin, for the chocolate motivation!

A  Novel

TOKYOPOP Inc.
5900 Wilshire Blvd. Suite 2000
Los Angeles, CA 90036

E-mail: info@TOKYOPOP.com
Come visit us online at www.TOKYOPOP.com

ISBN: 1-59816-444-9

First TOKYOPOP printing: March 2006
10 9 8 7 6 5 4 3 2 1
Printed in the USA

CONTENTS

GRAVITATION:
Character Profiles

Shuichi Shindou

Lead singer for the smash-hit pop band, Bad Luck. He's madly in love with his boyfriend, Yuki, despite the fact that Yuki is often cold and distant.

Eiri Yuki

An extremely attractive and uber-popular romance novelist. He's the kind of guy who always kept his heart walled-off--until he met Shuichi, that is.

Tohma Seguchi

Talented keyboardist for the legendary band, Nittle Grasper, and the young president of N-G Pro, Shuichi's record label.

K

Bad Luck's pistol-waving American manager.

Suguru Fujisaki

Bad Luck's calm and collected keyboardist.

Taki Aizawa

Ask's lead singer. He plots various schemes to try to sabotage Shuichi.

Hiroshi Nakano

Bad Luck's guitarist and Shuichi's best friend. His mom, dead-set against his music career, gives him lots of grief.

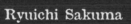

Ryuichi Sakuma

Nittle Grasper's genius vocalist and Shuichi's (physical and emotional) doppelganger.

Sakano

Bad Luck's hypertensive producer.

Prologue

He's as beautiful as an angel when he sleeps, Shuichi thought.

Yuki had perfectly smooth, pale skin, and dirty blond hair. Shuichi reached out and gently touched his handsome, almost androgynous face.

"You're only cute when you're sleeping," he whispered, tracing his knuckles down Yuki's angular cheek. Long black eyelashes fluttered briefly, but remained closed. Shuichi sighed softly.

Eiri Yuki had long since outgrown the description of "angel." Yuki was twenty-three years old, more than six feet tall, and weighed over a hundred and sixty pounds. He was one of the most attractive and talented novelists in the world, with legions of devoted female fans who devoured his love stories, making each one a best seller.

But his good looks were deceiving; he had a vicious streak a mile wide. Maybe he saved up all his sweet talk for his novels? Or perhaps he only used them to impress the ladies? Either way, whenever he spoke to Shuichi, every word that fell from his sensual lips was dagger-sharp.

At the moment, Yuki sprawled on the sofa in his study, asleep, unguarded. Naturally, Shuichi couldn't resist the desire to touch the older man.

"What gives you the right to be so damned beautiful?" he murmured, brushing soft, choppy hair off of Yuki's forehead. Yuki's usually cold, glaring brown eyes were now closed. This boosted Shuichi's courage.

"I hope you don't mind," he whispered, inching closer. His hand sank into the folds of the leather sofa as he leaned over, hovering just above Yuki's slightly parted mouth. *He told the world I was his lover, so this is okay, right?*

Shuichi's heart ached—he longed to press his mouth to Yuki's—but he suddenly froze up. His stomach clenched with guilt.

If I take advantage of him while he's asleep, and he wakes up in the middle of it, he'll hate me forever!

Yuki might look like an angel, but he could explode like a demon if anyone ever touched him unexpectedly. Shuichi had been on the receiving end of Yuki's wrath plenty of times to know it wasn't worth the risk.

Maybe just a little peck on the cheek? Then again, he might kick me out!

Shuichi trembled with sudden, irrational anger. He hesitated, holding his breath, trying to calm down. Yuki's body was like a holy temple to him; he didn't want to desecrate the sanctity of that. But just hovering over the couch was slightly uncomfortable. Sure, he had strong abs and a great lung capacity because of all those years of singing, but . . .

Why is my life filled with so many stupid dilemmas? This is all your fault, Yuki. You make me crave you, then you push me away!

Steeling himself, Shuichi decided to go for a kiss on Yuki's cheek. As he altered his course, he heard the voice that never failed to send a rush of pleasure up his spine.

"Just get it over with already."

"You're awake?" Shuichi scrambled backward, but Yuki grabbed his collar and pulled him close.

"Of course. I've been staring at my computer screen all day long. I just needed to rest my eyes."

"That's cheating!"

" 'Cheating?' What the hell do you mean?" Yuki asked calmly, ignoring Shuichi's glare.

Shuichi knew he was naïve at times, there was no denying that, but even *he* couldn't miss the mocking tone in Yuki's voice. His lover had laid himself out as bait, pretended to be asleep, and gotten Shuichi all worked up. But just as Shuichi was about to pounce, Yuki had pulled the rug out from under him. There was no doubt in Shuichi's mind that Yuki was simply toying with him, but he forgot his anger, distracted when Yuki's shirt opened slightly, revealing the older man's pale throat and broad chest.

"Um, yeah, you didn't do anything," Shuichi murmured absently.

"Of course not," Yuki said, tugging on a strand of Shuichi's hair.

"Yeah, you never *do* anything! I'm always the only one who—" But Shuichi's sullen outburst was cut short when Yuki yanked him closer. Their mouths met. Yuki's fingers tangled in his hair, scraped his scalp, and held him still. He parted Shuichi's lips and delved deep.

"Mm." The unexpected kiss left Shuichi speechless. His body slumped over like a rag doll. He nuzzled Yuki's chest, the once-crisp cotton brushing pleasantly against his cheek.

Yuki ruffled Shuichi's hair, laughed, and pushed him away.

"Who says I never do anything?" His smile was gentle, but there was a roguish twinkle in his eyes. "Satisfied now?" His words were harsh but his tone was amused.

Suddenly, Shuichi felt lonely and miserable. "Yuki," he whispered, staring at the older man intently.

Yuki raised an eyebrow. "If you want, we can keep going," he said with a smirk, stretching provocatively. "But it'll be your fault if I don't make my deadline."

He always left the decision up to Shuichi, always kept a little distance. Like Yuki could take him or leave him, and it wouldn't matter. He was coarse even when he was gentle—cold, yet passionate. Shuichi's mental map of Yuki had not changed a bit since they'd first met . . .

Before Shuichi's band, Bad Luck, had released its debut CD, he was an extremely frustrated and lost soul. Though Shuichi now devoted himself to singing, in those days, he still wrote the lyrics, the music, and the arrangements for all his songs.

It was the night before a big gig, and Shuichi had serious trouble with a song that just wouldn't *work*. Half-written lyrics in hand, he went for a walk in a nearby park. Frowning, he slowly meandered along secluded paths, wandering through patches of light.

"Believe in me," he whispered to himself.

His band partner and guitarist, Hiroshi Nakano, had taken one look at his latest song and told him, "I believe in you. You'll get it right. You've got talent." Hiro had said this lightly, smiling as always, but Shuichi knew he'd meant it; his best friend truly believed in him.

But Hiro's the one with the real talent. I don't know why he stays in a band with someone like me.

All their dreams were coming true, so why couldn't Shuichi just calm down and believe in himself? He'd heard it said that true genius was one percent inspiration, and ninety-nine percent perspiration. Everyone had some sort of talent, and deep down Shuichi knew his gift was for making great music.

"But I don't know how good a gift it is, or what to do with it," Shuichi grumbled, shuffling down a winding path. His confidence was as insubstantial as the shadows around him. He stopped. Suddenly, he felt like the trees were closing in on him, cutting him off from the world.

I have to stay positive.

He tried to imagine his bright future. Hiro and he would be rock stars! Bad Luck would rule the charts! Right?

He wanted to be optimistic, but it was too hard to do all by himself. Hiro always tried to cheer him up, and Shuichi was grateful that he had a partner who cared so much, but the other boy just wasn't enough. Shuichi needed someone . . . strong. Secure. Successful. He would be all right, if only he had someone special by his side believing in him.

"Maybe I should just go out and get a girlfriend," Shuichi murmured. *She could inspire and support me.* He started walking again.

"But no! That would be a lie. Love has to happen naturally." He broke into a sprint. "True love is the ultimate goal!"

He leapt forward and started to shinny up a lamppost. (Everyone had always said that spontaneously kicking his childlike energy into overdrive was one of his more unique character traits.)

He threw his head back and yelled, "Passion! Excitement! Loyalty! Without these, how can there be any love songs?"

Shuichi continued screaming from the top of the lamppost, "Shuichi Shindou, *this* is why you fail! This is why you can't write decent lyrics!"

As Shuichi cackled wildly, the autumn wind rushed through the trees and swept dry leaves around the empty park. Shivering, Shuichi came to his senses and slid carefully down the lamppost.

Sure, I could find someone to help me out of this rut. But if I don't figure out a way to get through this alone, then I'm no longer being true to myself.

Shuichi started walking again, his heart heavy.

He sneezed, and during that split second, he let go of his paper. The wind picked up his fragmented song and floated it farther down the path.

Aw, crap! Wiping his nose on the back of his hand, he ran after the paper. It flipped and twirled through the air, evading his grasp. Eventually, after a long chase, the paper landed. Shuichi froze, breathless.

A man so tall and pale that he simply had to be a foreigner stood there, clutching the precious scrap of paper. He looked like a model, wearing an expensive, tailored dark suit, sans tie. A cigarette dangled casually from the corner of his mouth. His hair was lustrous and his brown eyes were bright. This breathtaking figure, Shuichi would later learn, was Eiri Yuki.

Shuichi stared. It felt like time had stopped. He didn't remember walking forward. It was as if an immense force, like the current of a rushing river, tugged him toward the other man. They locked eyes, and Shuichi couldn't look away. Embarrassed, he reached out to retrieve his lyrics.

"Did you write this?" the man asked abruptly.

"Um," Shuichi hesitated, "yes."

"It's utter crap," the man spat at him. "You've obviously got zero talent." He turned on his heel to leave, and fired a parting shot: "Give up."

Shuichi went home on the verge of tears. The man's cruel rejection played over and over in his mind, flooding him with indignant rage, but in the end, he was able to turn that anger into motivation to finish the song. It was as if the stranger had lit a fire deep within him. He had to write the best song ever, become the number one idol in Japan, and make that arrogant man eat his words!

As time passed, despite his fury, Shuichi continued to feel that violent attraction. The man's words had been harsh and his manner had been absolutely frigid, but there had been something *else* too. Shuichi had seen devastating passion in the man's eyes. Strength. Confidence. It was baffling.

Instead of cursing him and hoping to never have to see him again, Shuichi felt like he just *had* to be near him. Like the stranger held his heart on a string. That feeling quickly grew, until Shuichi couldn't stand it anymore and took matters into his own hands. But he never once dreamed their chance encounter would result in his current relationship with Yuki . . .

Now he lived, fought, and slept with an infuriating, terrifying, mysterious angel.

"It's like a dream," Shuichi whispered as he lay in Yuki's arms, exhausted.

Ever since he'd met Yuki, Shuichi had regained his drive. Bad Luck had rocked that big gig, got signed to a major label, and released its premier single. Yuki had publicly used the word "lover" to refer to Shuichi, and there was no denying their intimate on-camera embrace. They made love often—and in very creative ways—so why did Shuichi feel like something was *missing?*

He stared at Yuki's face, searching for an answer.

Yuki's cheek twitched. "Don't drool when you look at me, idiot." Yuki tossed Shuichi off the sofa as easily as if he were pushing aside his bedcovers.

"Ow! You could be a bit nicer, you know."

"I've been nice enough for one evening. Or are you *still* not satisfied?" A quirked eyebrow told him what Yuki thought of that.

"Yeah, yeah . . . but when you didn't hold back, it hurt!" Shuichi grumbled, blushing, sprawled on the floor. "Even if it *was* good." He smiled sheepishly. Then he remembered the point he was trying to make. "For a romance novelist, you're really sucky at being romantic!"

Yuki's moods were whimsical, and although he had said they were lovers, he *still* kept quite a few girlfriends on the side. The two men were living together, but Yuki had set a week-by-week limit to that.

Nothing about their relationship felt solid. Shuichi's self-doubt ate at him, almost as strongly as it had before he'd met Yuki. But there was no going back; he could never be alone again. He just wanted to feel like they were *together*. He wanted to keep talking and touching the older man, feel connected, like they were in a real relationship, but he knew Yuki would get angry if he asked for more. Love had to come naturally, after all.

These thoughts were running through his head when he gazed at Yuki. The older man's clear eyes looked back at him coldly. They seemed to ask: *What are you wasting my time for? We're finished here. Move along.* Caustic but exquisite, Yuki took a long drag on his cigarette and turned away.

Shuichi sighed. *It's strange, but sometimes I think what I like best about him is this coldness. Yuki rarely if ever gives compliments. If I could just be worthy of his love . . . if my music could impress him . . . if he found me charming . . . then I'd know I was special.* Dejected, he stood to leave.

"Wait," Yuki said.

Shuichi spun around, surprised, but Yuki didn't continue. "You want a goodnight kiss?" Shuichi asked, puckering up in anticipation.

Yuki threw a dictionary at his head. "Don't fall asleep with your mouth open. You're a singer. You've got to protect your voice."

To anyone else, that statement would have sounded gruff and condescending, like a

parent's or a teacher's scolding, but Shuichi was touched.

"Yuki! You're worried about me! I promise I'll take good care of myself. Just you wait! Tomorrow's gonna be the best day ever!" Shuichi was so happy, he started hopping around, wiggling his hips. He barely heard Yuki's reply.

"I just don't want your boss yelling at me," Yuki said as he pushed Shuichi toward the door. "You need to take it easy." He shoved Shuichi across the threshold. "Night," he said, and slammed the door shut.

Shuichi stood outside the study, a dopey grin plastered on his face. Yuki toyed with, insulted, and rebuffed him on a daily basis, yet he had never felt happier . . . because his lover cared about him!

It's like we're two magnets, drawn together. No, it's like gravity—a force from which nothing can escape. Our attraction is like a raw stream of energy. But it's unpredictable, and its strength can't guarantee we'll stay together.

Shuichi's free-floating anxiety might have been an instinctual warning. He sensed danger, the way an animal could sense an approaching storm. Yuki seemed more standoffish these days, and Shuichi had a bad feeling about it . . .

Track One:
An Artist's Magnificent Life

"Good morning!" A spirited voice bounced around the recording studio's walls, echoing into the far reaches of the N-G Pro building. Shuichi Shindou, lead singer for the newly signed band, Bad Luck, greeted everyone in his path with a very enthusiastic, "Good morning!"

It was already well past noon, but in this industry, there was only one appropriate greeting.

"Good morning, Shuichi," everyone replied.

Shuichi was fairly scrawny for his age, but the boy bowing deeply to him was even smaller. Suguru Fujisaki was sixteen years old. He had joined Bad Luck after their grand debut. He was their keyboardist, and he arranged the group's music. He was calm, docile, and cute, but the gleam in his eyes also suggested he had a quick wit. Some people were fooled by Suguru's innocuous appearance and ended up underestimating him, though most people paid him all due respect. Shuichi, however, was an hyperactive island unto himself, and therefore always unaffected by Suguru's serious nature.

"Yo, Suguru! It's great to be young and alive! The sky's blue, the birds are singing, and good things are gonna happen!"

"Um, I don't see how those things correlate."

"You don't? But you're young! You'll understand someday! Be optimistic!" Shuichi shouted, punching his fist through the air. He shifted his gaze to the window and whispered, "I finally understand love. True love! It means looking out for one another."

"Uh . . . yeeeah." Suguru smiled weakly. They hadn't known each other for very long, and Suguru had yet to have a real conversation with Shuichi. He wasn't sure how to react to

Shuichi's non sequiturs and sudden outbursts of emotion.

But this wasn't the case for Shuichi's guitarist, Hiroshi Nakano. Gathering his long hair into a ponytail, Hiro smiled indulgently at Shuichi's antics.

"Hey, Shuichi," Hiro said. "Our debut single, 'The Power of Love,' is selling boatloads."

Shuichi threw his head back and cackled. "We've done it, Hiro! And tomorrow we'll hit another home run!"

Shuichi ran to Hiroshi and they high-fived, then struck a pose, shoulder to shoulder, and played the air guitar.

Back when they were still in elementary school, Hiro and Shuichi had both become addicted to the band Nittle Grasper, led by the virtuoso vocalist Ryuichi Sakuma. In junior high, Hiro and Shuichi had joined forces to start their own band. They played together all through high school, but it wasn't until they performed at their graduation ceremony that they were scouted out by a record label. They were sure it was nothing short of destiny that N-G Pro, operated by members of the very band that had been their inspiration, was the record company to sign them.

Such success was reason enough to dance for joy, but Hiro could sense something else had made Shuichi so ridiculously happy.

"Why the good mood?" Hiro asked. "Something happen with Yuki?"

"Ah . . . ha ha ha . . . Some things are better kept secret, even between friends." Shuichi's face turned bright red, leaving no doubt in Hiro's mind.

"Okay," Hiro said, nodding. "You're right." He averted his eyes, feigning nonchalance, comfortable playing the straight man to Shuichi's comedy act.

Shuichi grabbed Hiro's shoulder and dramatically pointed to the sky. "Look, Hiro—the sun, beautiful and bright. We've burst onto the Japanese charts like superstars, bringing warmth to the people, illuminating the otherwise dismal pop-rock scene for the betterment of society! How can we not be in a good mood?"

"From now on, the world is ours!" Hiro played along.

"Exactly!" Shuichi shouted, but then he lowered his voice and sat down on the floor. "Our concert psyched the crowd. I got to sing a duet with my idol, Ryuichi. We've been on TV." Shuichi clasped his arms around his knees. "Yuki and I are in love, and I'm just so happy." Shuichi twisted himself into a pretzel and murmured softly, "But it's all making me really scared."

Hiro nodded sympathetically. "They say a little pain comes with any good fortune."

"And here you are throwing water on my bliss!" Shuichi suddenly switched moods again, grinning and jumping up. "What are you, jealous?"

"Not at all," Hiro answered serenely. "I'm so happy for you and Yuki that I just could just take myself on a little spin 'round the Southern Islands."

Shuichi, always ready to leap aboard Hiro's evasions, adopted the tone of an elegant bar hostess. "I declare those are the crème de la crème of islands. I myself have only been to Hawaii, Bali, and Antarctica."

"Shuichi," Hiro said, unable to hold back his laughter. "Don't you think Antarctica's a bit *too* far south? Would be kind of cold. And it's more of a continent than an island!"

They struck another pose, standing shoulder to shoulder, and laughed heartily.

Suguru watched their antics from the other side of the room. *Why did I agree to join these two buffoons?* "That's it!" he shouted. "Enough!"

"What's up, Suguru?" Hiro asked.

"Relax man," Shuichi beamed. "Laugh a little."

Suguru inspected them carefully. Tohma Seguchi, the president of N-G Pro, had added him to Bad Luck to help convince the world they were serious musicians. Tohma believed in Suguru's talent and had entrusted him to whip the band into shape. Suguru had to keep Shuichi and Hiro focused and working hard.

"Shuichi, you mentioned that duet with Ryuichi," Suguru said calmly. "And it was a big success. But remember, you were opening for Ask."

"Who's Ask?" Shuichi responded blankly. His expression was so innocent that Suguru was at a loss for words.

"They're a band," Hiro said. "Remember? Debuted right before us? They're also with N-G Pro."

"Oh, yeah," Shuichi said. "I sorta remember some band playing before us. Annoying lead singer with droopy eyes?"

Hiro scrunched up his nose. "Yeah, that's the one. Droopy eyes."

"Droopy eyes aren't important!" Suguru declared, starting to lose his temper. "Every time we're on TV, we're on a comedy game show. Look, we're headed in the wrong direction. This is no time to be joking about the Arctic!"

"Ha ha! Nice one, Suguru," Shuichi declared. "We'll make a comedian of you yet!" He gave the younger boy a thumbs-up and a big smile.

"I wasn't trying to be funny. I mean it! This is no time for comedy." Suguru struggled to conceal his anger, talking through his teeth like a teacher lecturing an unruly student. "As long as you two act like a couple of comedians, that's the only kind of work we'll get. Nobody takes us seriously as musicians. For the life of me, I can't understand why Tohma is letting you two run wild. It makes you extremely hard to sell, and doesn't even begin to qualify as a publicity strategy."

Shuichi listened, slack-jawed. As soon as the conversation had turned somber, his higher brain functions switched off.

"Jeez, this boy is serious," Hiro whispered.

"This is a serious matter!" Suguru yelled, unable to hold back his frustration any longer. "We've got to aim for something higher!"

" 'Higher?' " Shuichi repeated, as if he'd never heard the word.

You mean like the New Year's music festival?" Hiro asked.

Suguru twitched. "Sure! Why not? My point is—something has to change. I'm part of this band now too, and I want us to improve as a group, *artistically*. We have the potential, but first we need to get people to listen to our music!"

Shuichi and Hiro sensed a strong drive behind Suguru's speech, notably different from their own ambitions.

"Suguru, you've got a lot of passion," Hiro said. "I think you're meant for more than just arrangements. You talk like a producer. You sound exactly like Tohma."

Suguru fell silent.

"Speaking of, where *is* the producer? And our manager?" Shuichi asked, as if he had not heard a single word Suguru had said. Without their producer or manager, they'd been behaving like students waiting for the bell to ring before class, but the fact was, they had a lot of work to do.

"Both were summoned to the president's office," Suguru said, wondering how he got so caught up with the other two that he forgot to mention it.

"Maybe we *have* been invited to the New Year's music festival," Shuichi said dreamily.

"If we have, I'll shave my head," Hiro laughed.

Suguru watched them closely. *Shuichi's a little more over the top than usual, but otherwise they seem normal. I wonder if the rumors are really true.*

Taki Aizawa, the lead singer of Ask, had been standing outside Bad Luck's studio, eavesdropping on Bad Luck's conversation by holding a glass against the door. *These chumps are so stupid. I bet their collective IQ is half of mine!*

He glared. When he had heard Shuichi describe him as the annoying singer with droopy eyes, Taki's grip on the glass tightened and his hand shook with anger.

How dare he make me a punch line?! Taki threw the glass to the floor. It shattered, but he still wasn't satisfied. He stomped on the shards with the heel of his boot, grinding the glass to dust, sniggering. *I'll make that bastard pay.* Suddenly, he heard someone approaching down the hall.

"I heard something break! Is anyone hurt?"

Bad Luck's producer, Sakano, came striding down the hallway, wearing an impeccably tailored suit. He was tall, lanky, and wore glasses. When he got to the door, the hallway was empty. Taki had made a swift exit, but Sakano noticed the broken glass all over the floor. He whipped out a handkerchief from his breast pocket and began cleaning it up.

"Who would do such a thing? People are animals! The studio isn't a bar."

Sakano had finished cleaning the floor when he saw a streak of grease on the door. He licked his thumb and started to wipe it clean.

"I just don't understand! Why can't people keep things tidy?"

Suddenly, the door was yanked open from the inside, and Sakano fell over into the meeting room. "Aaiieee!"

Ignoring the fact that his producer lay on the floor, Shuichi held the door open and said brightly, "Good morning! You're late. I was leaving to go looking for you."

Sakano hauled himself up. "Good morning, everyone." He bowed low, one finger holding his now-bent glasses to his face. "I'm so sorry. The meeting with the president dragged on quite a bit longer than expected."

"What meeting?" Hiro asked.

It was a straightforward question, but Sakano jumped as if he'd seen a ghost.

He wavered back and forth for a few seconds, unsure of what to say. Then he clapped his hands together. "Why don't we have some tea?"

The members of Bad Luck flopped down into their chairs and watched Sakano as he ran to a side table where an electric kettle, a teapot, some tea leaves, rice crackers, and several teacups lay on a serving tray.

Shuichi and the others waited patiently as Sakano got busy. Although he was their producer, not their manager, everyone had agreed to let him make tea since it seemed like the only thing that calmed him down. And since their actual manager didn't know how to make Japanese tea, it worked out perfectly.

Once they were all sipping their drinks contentedly, Suguru asked, "So, what was the meeting about?"

"Oh, um, you know. This and that," Sakano said timidly. "Um, you know, plans for your future. The trivial details of business."

"Sakano!" Suguru interrupted. "Stop waffling! If you're not gonna step up and handle things, there's no reason for me to be here. I won't compromise when it comes to my music. I've had enough with this comedy musician nonsense! I'm an artist. *We're* artists, and as artists our goal should be to conquer the music industry!"

"Magnificent!" Sakano raced to Suguru's side and grabbed his hand. Tears started streaking down his cheeks like raindrops on a windowpane. "For a moment, I thought I was listening to the president! Such confidence! Such determination!" Sakano was so enraptured, he couldn't see anyone other than Suguru. "You speak the truth! We'll launch a tour from the Tokyo Dome, or the Budohkan, and from then on, we'll play every stadium in the country!"

"That sounds very good," Suguru said with a smile, utterly composed. He kneeled down in front of Sakano. "Make it happen, Producer!"

Sakano looked about to faint from joy.

"Yeah," Hiro said, "but really, we don't need anything more than a concert hall."

"I'll do anything as long as people get to hear our music," Shuichi added.

Suddenly, a ceiling panel came crashing down into the middle of the room. A man plunged down after it, landing in a cloud of dust. He had blue eyes and long blond hair that was tied back in a ponytail. His name was K, and he was well known in the industry as the psychotic manager from America. He was dressed in full combat gear, and gripped a machine gun gingerly in his right hand. Shuichi lay on the floor next to him, having been pummeled during the cave in. K brushed his shoulders clean, scattering dust and debris into Shuichi's eyes.

"Now that *I'm* your manager, Carnegie Hall, the Sydney Opera House, and the Kokugikan are all at your fingertips."

"But the Kokugikan is for sumo wrestling," Hiro said, unperturbed by K's dramatic entrance. Suguru and Sakano stood beside him with their mouths gaping open, totally flabbergasted.

K smiled widely. "I knew that! Never mind. Just an American joke."

"Where the hell did you come from?!" Shuichi shouted. He tried to grab the front of K's shirt to lift himself up, but the American was too tall. Finally, K saw Shuichi struggling and so he picked the singer up by the scruff of his collar, as if Shuichi was a kitten.

K laughed. "Ha ha ha! You mean you didn't see? I came from the *tendon*."

Everyone frowned. *The tempura bowl?*

Shuichi held up a finger. "You mean, the *tenjo?*" *The ceiling?*

"Ah, right. My mistake." He patted Shuichi on the head with the hand that wasn't holding his gun. "My job is to protect this company's talent. I was on patrol, looking for spies, assassins, and terrorists."

"In . . . the . . . ceiling?" Sakano asked nervously.

"Of course! That's where *all* the spies are in Japan." He proudly puffed out his chest.

After a long silence, they began furiously whispering to each other.

"All right, who showed him a ninja movie?" Shuichi asked.

"Someone really ought to tell him that there aren't any ninjas in the twenty-first century!" Hiro said. "There's nothing up there but roaches and mice."

"Don't we have more important things to discuss?" Suguru asked impatiently.

"Oh, right." Sakano straightened up, fixed his glasses, and mustered his most authoritative tone. "K, tell them about their next job."

"Roger!" K saluted and holstered his weapon. "I've got a very creative job for you!"

They awaited K's next words with a mixture of anticipation and unease.

"I know how you guys love to be on TV. So, you'll be the special guests on next week's episode of *Sing! Dance! Bonbaban!*"

An awkward silence followed. It was exactly what they had feared.

"Something wrong?" K cocked his head to one side.

"How many times do we have to tell you?" Shuichi asked. "We're a *band!* Not some silly comedians!"

"But it's *Sing! Dance!*" Everyone glared at the foreigner. K's hand twitched, reaching reflexively toward his holster.

"Yes, yes, but we won't get to perform," Hiro quickly explained. "We'll be expected to sing and dance while playing silly games and making the audience laugh."

"Jeez, Japanese sure is difficult!" K said, throwing up his hands.

"Acting like you're fresh off the boat won't help you now!" Hiro said.

K shrugged. "Uh, look guys, it's TV. It's a chance to sell your faces to the average Joe."

Sakano and Suguru sighed, their shoulders sagging dejectedly.

In a meeting room after business hours, Sakano and K faced each other across the table, both wearing grim expressions. The sky outside had darkened, and inside, most of the lights were off.

"Did you find anything?" Sakano asked.

"No. No cameras, no bugs, nothing I didn't put there myself."

"Then it must be someone on the inside . . ."

Earlier that day, they had both been summoned to the president's office and informed that someone had leaked information about Bad Luck to the public—information that nobody outside of N-G Pro could have known. Tohma had instructed K to do a thorough inspection of the building, but K had found nothing. They were left to assume that the source was someone within the company.

"Of course, the secret in question," Sakano began, "it isn't true, is it?"

"Doesn't matter. True or not, someone's trying to destroy Bad Luck, and it's my job to nip their plan in the bud." K stroked his gun lovingly. "We do not bow down to the enemy!"

"Darn samurai movies," Sakano muttered. "We just have to keep our eyes open, all right?"

"Okay."

As they walked into the corridor, K noticed a tiny glimmer of light by his foot. He reached down to inspect it and stood back up holding a sliver of broken glass up to his eyes.

"I sense criminal activity!"

His blue eyes flashed like a hunter who had found the tracks of his prey.

"I'm home!" Shuichi shouted as he walked into Yuki's place, exhausted. He made a beeline for the study, where he thought Yuki would be working hard to meet his deadline.

"Yuki?" The lights were out, and the computer was turned off. He checked the kitchen, the bathroom, and the bedroom, but there was no sign of Yuki anywhere. He looked out the window and noticed that Yuki's car was missing from the parking lot.

"I rushed home for nothing."

He plunked himself down on the floor to wait and flicked on the TV. The room filled with music. His heart raced. Nittle Grasper was playing his absolute favorite song, "Be There."

"I can't believe it! Thank goodness I came straight home!"

He thrust himself so close to the screen that he could feel the warmth of the TV radiate over his face as his eyes devoured his idol, Ryuichi Sakuma.

Ryuichi had a boyish body and a fresh face despite his thirty-one years, but his voice was so powerful that it seemed to come from someone ten times his size. His voice was so beautiful, it could tear hearts wide open with a single note.

"He's so damn cool."

Shuichi stared obsessively at Ryuichi, the man he'd imitated every day since childhood. During the denouement, Ryuichi talked about the years he'd spent in America following the breakup of his band. But he said he was back in Japan now to reunite Nittle Grasper and play at the Fly to the Next Century music festival.

"Dude! Ryuichi! I am *so* there!" Shuichi moaned, unable to bear the thought of having to wait so long to see Ryuichi onstage. *But wait! We work for the same record label now!* (They had even performed a duet together. Shuichi lost himself while reliving that glorious moment. He had dreamed about it for so many years that he couldn't believe it when it had actually happened.)

Then the song resumed, and Shuichi suddenly found himself on the verge of tears. This piece had always made his heart soar, but now Ryuichi's silken voice left him feeling unexpectedly heartbroken. *Is it because Yuki isn't here to share it with me?*

On the television, Ryuichi laughed as the fans demanded more. For a man normally so childish, he gave off an almost regal air sometimes. *The aura that only the chosen ones have.*

Shuichi continued to feel awful after the program ended. He turned off the TV and dragged himself to his feet. Yuki still wasn't home.

"Where could he be? He has a deadline. That slacker!" Suddenly, he was gripped by jealousy. "He better not be cheating on me!"

At that moment, seeing his lover seemed like the most important thing in the world. It felt unbearably lonely sitting by himself on the sofa, where they had made love just the night before, so Shuichi plunked himself down in front of Yuki's computer. But even there, not a trace of his lover's warmth remained. Shuichi let out a desperate sigh.

"Hey, you," he said to the computer. "*You know where he is, right? He pays attention to you. I've got no idea. Maybe a really fancy clothing store, or a five-star restaurant?*"

Shuichi didn't know what Yuki did in his free time or what kinds of places he frequented. All Shuichi knew about Yuki was his name and occupation, and how skilled he was when they made love. Did that mean that they weren't really a couple?

Labels aren't important! Shuichi had fallen in love with Yuki before he even knew his name.

Shuichi hadn't even realized that the strong tug he felt was *called* love, until Yuki pointed it out to him. But it was true. He was in love, and he yearned for Yuki with his entire body and soul. *Isn't that enough? What more do I need to know?*

But Shuichi hesitated. Even after all this time, was Yuki really his?

He felt empty. He let his eyes wander around the room. It was sparsely furnished and obsessively organized. The sleek furniture and modern decorations looked expensive, but Shuichi couldn't tell for sure. What he *did* know was that it matched Yuki's personality. Yuki never spoke a needless word, and he could wear a plain, simple dress shirt and still look sexy. Everything about Yuki was functional, classy, and sophisticated.

When Shuichi thought about it, it was unbelievable that Yuki had let him in this room at all, and it was truly miraculous that Yuki had let Shuichi move into the apartment. Just thinking about it made Shuichi feel like skipping down the street, singing and dancing with glee.

"Maybe I'm too greedy," Shuichi whispered, perusing the finely crafted bookshelves that held all of Yuki's published works. "Am I?" he asked the books, but they didn't answer.

I want to know more about you, Yuki. I want to get right inside of you, but you've built a wall around yourself, a thick, impenetrable barrier that keeps me from getting closer.

Shuichi sighed. *If I thought I could break it down, I'd do it in a second. But I can't. I'm afraid that if I try, you'll turn against me. Or even worse, I'm afraid that I'll hurt you in the process, and then I wouldn't be able to live with myself.*

"What's wrong with me?"

Shuichi wasn't the kind of guy who worried about these sorts of things. He wasn't used to thinking things through. He had always just done whatever he wanted, without considering the consequences. But Shuichi wasn't alone anymore. Being in love complicated everything.

His cell phone rang, startling Shuichi out of his reverie. His ringtone was the same Nittle Grasper song that had just been playing on TV.

"Yuki?!" he blurted out, his hand gripping the phone with such force it was liable to break.

"What, not a good time?" It was his sister, Maiko—not exactly whom he'd hoped. Her voice was carefree and annoying.

"Dammit, just Maiko," he mumbled.

"Damn yourself. Why didn't you tell me about this breaking up crap?"

"Breaking up? Oh, you mean Nittle Grasper? Yeah, they broke up, but they just announced they're getting back together." Shuichi smiled.

"Shuichi!" she screamed. "You're making me dizzy!" Like her brother, she could get worked up very easily. "This is no time to be thinking about *other* bands!"

"What? Why?"

"Why? Because Bad Luck is breaking up! I just read it on the 'net."

"What? How could . . . Nobody told me! What's K doing?" Shuichi was genuinely shaken, but then he snapped out of it. "Don't worry about it. We're not breaking up. We're lining up new work. We're gonna be on *Sing! Dance! Bonbaban!* K's even talking about playing a show at the Kokugikan."

"The sumo hall? Odd. So, it's all a load of crap? Like, just some idiot making things up? I mean, it wasn't in any legit magazine or anything. My boyfriend told me about it, so I thought I'd call, you know, and make sure it wasn't true."

She sounded relieved, but Shuichi started to feel anxious. *If the rumors seem real enough that even my own sister believes them . . .*

Maiko laughed. "Hey, sorry to bug you about nothing. You know, it also said something about Hiro leaving the band to study for his college entrance exams . . ."

"Yeah, but that was a long time ago, right before we graduated high school." At the mere mention of Hiro's absence, all of the angst Shuichi had felt during those weeks came rushing back.

Hiro had decided to hang up his guitar and live the secure life his mother had always wanted for him. Shuichi had felt angry and abandoned because he didn't understand the inner conflict

Hiro had been going through. But Hiro changed his mind and came back to Bad Luck. *Hiro! You are way too good for me! You gambled your own future on someone like me! I hope we'll be together forever.*

While these emotions flooded through him, his sister chatted away.

"But he ended up failing the test, right? Then you guys did that gig at graduation where you got scouted, then signed and released. There's no way he'd quit now."

The rumors can't be true! Just today, they'd vowed to go on TV, boost their sales, and launch a national tour.

"So how's it going with the *other* thing? You know, Mom still thinks you're living alone. She'd probably have a heart attack or something if she knew you were shacking up with a man! And if she heard that man was Eiri Yuki! I know *I'm* jealous."

"Shut up a minute, all right?" Shuichi roared into the phone. "I can't think!"

"Hey! Don't shout at me! I'm just trying to help!"

Shuichi didn't hear her because he was already lost in thought. Now he understood how Yuki felt. *Do I really talk that much? I guess so! Must be why he's always telling me to shut my trap. That's why he yells at me. That's why he leaves the house when he knows I'm coming home. Maybe he hates me . . . ?*

"Oh, man!" he cried, unable to rein in his agitation.

On the other end, Maiko started to worry that there was something to the rumors after all. "You're not really breaking up, are you?"

"Of course not! We love each other too much for that!"

"Right, right. You and Hiro are like brothers."

"Huh? Oh, the band." Shuichi struggled to untangle his thoughts, cursing himself for getting bogged down about Yuki. *I don't deserve to be Hiro's partner.*

"Don't be silly! Hiro's never gonna quit," Shuichi said, attempting to be lighthearted for Maiko's sake. "He's my one and only guitarist.

Together, we're gonna rule the whole world—the whole universe!"

"Well, okay, don't get carried away." She laughed.

"Yeah, yeah. Look, I gotta go. Brush your teeth, do your homework, and be nice to Mom!" Shuichi signed off cheerfully, wriggling out of further conversation. "Bye!"

The moment he hung up, his body felt drained of energy, and he gave way to depression. *What's up with these Internet rumors? It just doesn't make sense. We're doing so well, why would we be breaking up?*

He knew it was just a lot of hot air, but it really bothered him that these kinds of lies were being spread about *his* band. He wanted to share these feelings with Yuki, to get them off of his chest, so he could relax, but Yuki still wasn't home.

Shuichi hugged his arms around his legs and waited, but after a while, when Yuki *still* hadn't come home or even called, he began to sulk.

"You're supposed to be my lover. That means you're there for me when I need to be cheered up."

Shuichi glared at the computer. It seemed able to wait for Yuki patiently.

"Maybe," he said to the computer, "no, *definitely*—you get to spend more time with him than I do." He reached out and touched the keyboard. "Yuki's fingers have touched these keys . . . the same hands that moved across my body have moved across these buttons. And I bet he's shown you his true face, told you the deepest secrets he hides in his heart."

Shuichi grabbed the computer and shook it violently. "Trade places with me! I wanna be with Yuki all day! I wanna know how he feels!"

Just as he threw his arms around the computer, something hard hit him in the back of the head before falling to the floor with a thump.

"Getting turned on by the computer? Creepy."

Shuichi spun around to see his sweetheart standing in the doorway.

"Yuki! Where have you been? I was so worried about you!" With tears streaming down his cheeks, Shuichi ran up to Yuki and hugged him tightly, like a lost child reunited with his mother.

Yuki didn't hug back. He just rubbed the back of his neck in irritation. "I went to buy that." He pointed to the package that he had just flung at Shuichi. "Printer paper."

He sure was gone an awfully long time! "If only you'd told me! I could've saved you a trip and picked some up on my way home."

"I felt like a break." He flung Shuichi off and headed for his desk.

Shuichi stared at Yuki's back. It seemed to be saying: *it's time for you to leave; time for work.*

Pain welled up in Shuichi's heart. *For Yuki, I'm just something that can be tossed aside without a second thought.* "Hey," Shuichi said.

"What?" Yuki turned.

His brown eyes gazed down at Shuichi and, like always, there wasn't a trace of kindness in them.

Shuichi was familiar with that glare; he always pretended that it was a loving gaze. But at least this time, Yuki was actually listening.

"Nothing . . ." There were so many things he wanted to ask, but they all suddenly seemed unimportant. *All I need is for you to look at me.* Desire suddenly welled up inside Shuichi, threatening to break his fragile happiness.

"Well, if you've got nothing to say, then shut up."

That really hurt. "Hey, you don't hate me, do you?" Shuichi thought he saw Yuki's gaze sharpen, if only by a fraction.

"Stop wasting my time with stupid questions."

"Right. Um. Good luck with work," he said and bolted out of the room.

Stupid? What's that mean? Did he mean don't ask something I know the answer to? So, he doesn't hate me? Or . . . Did he mean that his contempt should be obvious?

Oh! Yuki! Why won't you just tell me how you feel? I don't want to piss you off, but I just don't know . . . I'm an idiot!

Alone in the hall, real tears stung Shuichi's eyes. If only he had turned as he was leaving and seen Yuki's face, he would have known the answer to his question.

"What was that about?" Yuki lit a cigarette. He didn't understand Shuichi's question, or why he had snapped in response. *Some romance novelist I am.* He exhaled sharply.

A shapeless cloud of smoke drifted in front of his beautiful face before dissipating into nothing.

Track Two:
The Plot to End Bad Luck

"Stupid Maiko, giving me weird-ass dreams." Shuichi boarded the train without even bothering to stifle his yawn. It was well past rush hour, so only a few people were forced to stand.

"What a weird dream! Hiro was wearing bottle-thick glasses, studying feverishly," Shuichi said to himself as he sat down. "Even had a headband with 'Must Pass!' written on it." He giggled to himself.

Two women dressed like secretaries were sitting next to Shuichi. They glanced in his direction and whispered to each other with their

hands over their mouths. At first, Shuichi didn't hear them. If he had, he would've realized that they thought he was very cute, but crazy.

Eventually, he noticed the women and stopped talking to himself. *I must look nuts.* In fact, on the way to the station, he'd noticed more than a few people staring at him. *Bad Luck isn't that widely known yet, but maybe it's time I started to act more like a celebrity.*

Shuichi glanced ahead of him, trying his best to look calm and collected. His eyes landed on the passenger across from him, a young businessman who was reading a newspaper. Shuichi couldn't help but read the headlines. He just skimmed them absentmindedly until his eyes caught on the words "Breaking Up Already."

Another band about to fall apart. Must be a common rumor.

Shuichi leaned in to get a better look, but the businessman, sensing Shuichi's interest, folded the newspaper so he couldn't see. But his plan backfired, since what Shuichi was trying to read ended up right on top.

"Hiroshi Nakano Leaving to Study Medicine?"

Man, that guy has the same name as Hiro. And Hiro was thinking of med school, too. He chuckled to himself silently, but then it clicked. He grabbed the newspaper, howling, "What? What?!"

"Hey, let go!" The businessman tried to grab his paper back.

"Hiroshi Nakano, guitarist for Bad Luck? This is about us!"

"Sorry. I don't know anything about it," the businessman apologized, thinking Shuichi was crazy, but this only made matters worse.

"Why don't you know? It's your paper!"

"I didn't *write* it!" The poor man, unable to handle the suddenly furious stranger, let go of the newspaper. "Uh . . . this is my stop." He jumped up and was almost out the door when he said, "Keep it!"

"Thanks," Shuichi muttered. Beside him, the two secretaries whispered excitedly.

"I think it's really him. It's Shuichi Shindou from Bad Luck."

"Such a shame! They were good and just getting started. No wonder he's gone crazy."

Shuichi wondered if the attention he'd gotten on the way to the station was because of this article.

"Oh, man," Shuichi mumbled, staring in horror at the crumpled newspaper. Some of the other passengers began whispering about Shuichi as the train pulled out of the station.

The door burst open and slammed against the wall with such force that it nearly broke off of its hinges, but Hiro just smiled as Shuichi came hurtling into the studio.

"What the hell is this? 'Hiroshi Nakano, guitarist for Bad Luck?' "

"What's up, Shuichi?" Hiro greeted him as if he always burst in that way. "You're late."

"Thanks to you!" Shuichi grabbed Hiro furiously. "Because of you, I forgot to get off the train, ended up who knows where, and got yelled at by the newsstand lady for not buying the magazine I was reading while I waited for a train going the other direction!"

"What's going on, man? Have a fight with Yuki or something?"

Shuichi had a hand on each of Hiro's shoulders and kept shaking him violently. Hiro kept beaming, so he shook Hiro twice as hard.

"Shuichi! Calm yourself, please!" Sakano flung his arms around Shuichi like he was trying to save Hiro from a rabid animal. "Let go of him!"

"I'm never letting go of Hiro!"

"Good morning!" Suguru entered the room, took one look at the bizarre spectacle before him, and stopped in his tracks.

Shuichi growled like an animal as he shook Hiro violently. Sakano clung to Shuichi's waist, crying, trying to ride out the storm. Through all of this, Hiro just grinned.

"Suguru," Hiro said, his voice calm and natural. "Don't just stand there, come on in."

The spell broken, Suguru flung down the magazine he had been holding. "I suppose *this* is why you've all gone crazy?" he asked angrily.

The article was the same one Shuichi had seen in the newspaper, the same one he'd read at the newsstand.

"Reading that made you late?" Hiro asked Shuichi. "You could've just borrowed it from Suguru."

"Quit trying to worm out of this!" Shuichi dropped to his knees, his hands still clutching Hiro's legs. "Leaving the band to take a test? You have any idea how that makes me feel?" Shuichi's eyes brimmed with tears as he looked up at Hiro.

Although Shuichi had laughed off the rumors when Maiko had called the night before, when he saw them printed in the magazine, his old fear of abandonment returned.

"Why?" Sakano sobbed. "Why didn't you tell us?" He was sprawled on the floor where Shuichi had flung him. Now he sat upright, gnashing his handkerchief in his teeth, his right hand fluttering to his chest in an effeminate way. "Am I so unreliable?"

"Yup."

"Really?" Sakano looked at them.

"Yeah." All three nodded.

The producer collapsed in a sobbing heap. "I know. I know. But you could have talked to the president or to K! You could have told *someone!*"

"Don't worry about it," snapped Shuichi, standing. "It's old news. This all happened before we signed!"

Surprised, Sakano stopped crying. "What?"

Hiro nodded, smiling from ear to ear. "Yup. Someone just dug up an old fight we had a long time ago, before we were scouted."

"But . . . Shuichi was . . ." Sakano wiped his tears away.

Shuichi scratched his head and offered Sakano a sheepish grin. "Oh, you know. Like, everything just came flooding back to me. I just got a little carried away."

"Carried away?!" Again, Sakano collapsed on the floor with a grand flourish. "You enjoyed watching us, didn't you, Hiro? And you too, Shuichi. You enjoyed it a lot. Too much!"

"Sorry," Hiro said. "But it was funny seeing Shuichi so upset about it."

"So, you aren't angry?" Shuichi asked. "I mean, I didn't believe the rumors, but still . . . I'm sorry."

"Don't apologize. You did what you did because you still need me. And that just makes me glad."

"Oh, Hiro," Shuichi said. They stared lovingly into each other's eyes.

Sakano, in a voice filled with deep envy, said, "So the two of you were just confirming your friendship, and I made the mistake of getting in the way."

"Sakano," Hiro said, "don't sulk. It was all a farce. Let's get some work done."

Shuichi helped Sakano up off of the floor as Hiro watched, smirking broadly.

Suguru peered at them, just as he'd been doing throughout the commotion. Rather than get involved in their chaos, he had secretly wanted to run away. "So, there's no problem?" Suguru asked, just to be sure.

Hiro nodded. "All settled. At least, for my part."

"But why didn't you contact the magazine and let them know the rumors were false?" Suguru asked.

"Think about it," Hiro said. "If we confirm or deny one rumor, we'll have to confirm or deny them all. Between the three of us, which member of this band has the biggest story to hide?"

Instead of answering, Suguru turned to look at Shuichi.

"Yup." Hiro nodded. "The fact that Shuichi's lover is a man, not to mention, the best-selling novelist, Eiri Yuki. It's a major scandal." Hiro swallowed. "So I get everyone focused on me. They can dig all they want, but there's no dirt to be found. I'm still single, and I was a straight-A student. All they'll end up with is this kind of silly story."

"I still can't believe it," Suguru said gravely.

"Believe what?"

"That Tohma would allow anyone to get close to Yuki, much less keep quiet when one of his clients gets involved with him romantically." Tohma's wife was Yuki's older sister, and her love for her brother was far more intense than the average sibling's. She believed the world revolved around Yuki.

"Let's pray that he doesn't get involved," Hiro said. "Because I don't care if he's the president, I'd never stand by while someone made Shuichi cry."

There was a hint of steel in Hiro's voice that made Suguru turn back around, but when he did, he found Hiro smiling as usual.

After the meeting, Suguru went upstairs to Tohma's office.

"I can't shake it from my mind. Hiro made a point of saying it was settled 'as far as I'm concerned.' But I think that maybe the article was partially true, that maybe his mother *is* opposed to his music career."

Tohma rebuked the young man without bothering to look up from his paperwork. "Hiroshi Nakano is under contract with N-G Pro. As long as he doesn't try to break it, there's no problem. It's nothing, just some free publicity for Bad Luck."

Tohma swiveled his chair to gaze out of his large window. His office was on the top floor, and he had an expansive view of the city. Tokyo teemed with the chaotic movement of people and cars; everything flowed through the streets like rushing water. It was a very simple thing to control that flow, similar to creating a band and making their records sell. All you had to do was build the right infrastructure—plan well. A traffic signal here, a highway there, and people would do exactly what you wished them to do.

But the problems came after that. A well-planned city would draw an influx of people; a successful band would draw hundreds of thousands of fans. New problems would arise, and more work would have to be done. The bigger the success, the bigger the obstacles. That is, unless you had an unparalleled talent like that of Ryuichi Sakuma, a shooting star who could soar above those obstacles without even realizing they existed.

Ryuichi had the innate ability to overcome the odds with little effort. He possessed tremendous charisma, and that convinced people to open paths for him. He was resourceful enough to fight his way though tough times, and, most elusive of all, he had good luck. True talent was the combination of all these things. The initial sales were the work of the promoters. The ongoing sales relied upon the strength of his products.

Tohma spun back around, wearing a cherubic, carefree smile. He resembled Suguru slightly, though he was more mature and relaxed. He was handsome and fresh-faced enough to pass for a high school student, though he was already in his thirties. And although he looked childishly earnest, he was wiser than a veteran politician.

"If the rumors crush them, then that's all they were worth," Tohma said.

They were fearsome words, said in such a casual tone that Suguru felt chills.

Outside the window, a small bird flew by, riding the turbulent wind effortlessly.

"But if they're the real thing," Suguru said, "they'll use these rumors like a tailwind and soar."

Unaware that he was being discussed elsewhere, Hiro made his way home. He had moved out the moment he'd graduated and was living alone in his own private castle: a small but efficient room that he rented. He pressed the button on his answering machine, and a familiar, high-pitched voice filled the room.

"Hiro, quit that band and go to college. You had good grades. It's not too late. I'll pay for—" *Beep*.

"Think about your future. You don't want to end up wasting your life like your brother. Your father and I are very—" *Beep*.

"Why aren't you home yet? What can be taking so long? You're just in a rock and roll group. You can't have very much to—" *Beep*.

None of her messages finished within the time the machine allowed. There were ten more messages on the machine, some with just a dial tone. While Hiro was changing, his mother's increasingly hysterical voice echoed in his tiny room. He had been able to maintain a sunny smile the entire time he was at the studio, but now his face went slack. He pulled his hair free from his bandana, and shook it out.

"I talked this out with her after graduation. I *told* her this was my path," he mumbled with more than a hint of frustration. He deleted the messages on his answering machine then he deleted all the messages on his cell phone.

The doorbell rang, followed by the sounds of someone coming in.

Oh crap! She's here! He had wanted to avoid a head-on collision with his mother, and had been trying to get her to understand things by talking on the phone. Combing his fingers through his hair, he slowly turned toward the door, preparing himself for an argument, but to his relief, it wasn't his mother.

"Ciao," Hiro's older brother, Yuji Nakano, said. He smiled.

"Yuji!"

"Your door wasn't even locked. I could've been an axe murderer." Yuji chuckled, locking the deadbolt behind him. Yuji looked relaxed and happy, despite having been branded a "waste of a life" by his parents.

"Dude, what's the point of having a cell phone if you never answer it?"

"Yeah, I know," Hiro said. "So, what's up? Did your audition go well?"

"No. Ouch." Yuji staggered backward as if stabbed. "I'm still working on that world record for rejections." Yuji was an actor—or at least, a currently unemployed aspiring actor. "Thought we could get drunk together. Just got some severance pay from my last temp job."

He started pulling beer cans and snacks out of a plastic bag. It crackled and rustled. After Hiro cleaned off the table, the actor and the musician, fresh from making their parents cry, knocked their beer cans together in a toast.

"To Yuji's world record!"

"To Hiro's first time gracing the cover of a tabloid!"

Hiro jerked back, spraying beer in a graceful arc that landed right on Yuji's face. It dripped down onto the coffee table.

"Crap, dude." Yuji frowned.

"Sorry. But it's your fault, saying something like that out of the blue." He grabbed a towel and flung it to his older brother.

Yuji wiped his face, laughing. "I'm the one who was surprised. I didn't think you were *that* famous."

"I'm not. Not for my music, at least. We're not respected as musicians. We're treated like comedians on those stupid games shows and silly variety programs."

"So modest!" Yuji opened a second can and started to chug it.

Hiro had barely touched his first, swirling the beer around and around. "I mean it."

"Not having fun?"

"Well, as long as I can play music with Shuichi . . ."

"Then why worry?" Taking his own advice, Yuji started on his third beer. He guzzled it down loudly.

Hiro sat silently, watching his brother polish the drink off. He wanted to appear on a music program for Shuichi's sake. He simply wanted as many people as possible to hear Shuichi sing. Hiro also wanted desperately for his mother to give him her blessing. Of course, it didn't really change anything if she refused, but he couldn't bear the thought that she didn't respect him or Shuichi.

"Oh, yeah, I forgot," Yuji said, turning his attention away from his beer for a moment. "This buddy of mine asked me to be in his play. Tiny theater, no budget, but still, it's something."

"I'll help you sell tickets. I can take them by the studio."

"Thanks. It's gonna be great. We're really killing ourselves in rehearsals."

Yuji looked so pleased, Hiro couldn't help but wish him all the best. He envied his brother's ability to live his own life without needing anyone's approval.

"Good for you." Hiro raised his can.

"Right back at you."

They toasted each other's happiness.

Hiro grinned happily. His brother knew him well and had always been supportive of his dreams. When Bad Luck released its first single, Yuji had come by to celebrate. But Yuji had also understood that it was just the beginning, so they toasted not to the CD release, but to the future. Now all Hiro had to do was get his mother to understand just how important a career in music was to him.

Yuji was drunk and sprawled on the floor, on the verge of passing out. Hiro tossed a futon cushion at him.

"Sorry, Hiroshi."

"We're brothers."

"No, I'm not sorry I'm spending the night. I mean, I can't do anything right, so Mom gave up on me and put all her hopes on you. That's why I'm sorry."

Hiro shrugged. "You've got nothing to apologize for."

"Just put up with it a little longer. She's just in a state of shock or something. She never thought you'd turn your back to her, and she doesn't want to admit you're right."

Hiro plunked himself down next to Yuji. "So actors *are* good at reading other people's emotions."

"If I'm so great, then why can't I land a decent audition?" Yuji chuckled.

"I thought if the band became successful, she'd get on board and stop bad-mouthing Shuichi. But how big do we have to be before that happens?"

Yuji shook his head, then threw his arm around Hiro. "See, your value systems are all different. There's no telling if she'll ever see you as a success. If only she could understand that you're happy."

Hiro snuggled closer. "Even if she never understands," he said, "I'm satisfied. It's just that I know Shuichi really lets this kind of thing get to him. For his sake, I want to clear things up."

Hiro was silent for a moment. *I won't let anyone make Shuichi cry. Not my mom, not even the man that Shuichi loves. If it ever came down to it . . .*

"You know what?" Hiro said, trying to calm himself down.

"What?"

"We're a bit too big to be sharing a futon. Makes me kinda sad."

"Really? I'm happy!"

"Because you're drunk," Hiro said, smiling, his eyes closing.

All I ever need is to play music with Shuichi. That's always going to be enough for me. As for Shuichi, I want him to be able to fling himself headlong into anything he likes, without worrying about anything else.

"Did I forget to bring the album with me?" Shuichi looked around his apartment for the first time in a long while. He hardly ever came here anymore, and the place was a complete mess. Random parts of old synthesizers were scattered everywhere, making the place look like a miniature junkyard.

Shuichi was looking for an old photo album because of his upcoming appearance on

Sing! Dance! Bonbaban! The TV show needed childhood photos of its guests for one of the games they had planned.

"I don't remember packing it, so it must still be at home." But he kept looking just in case, poking through the mountains of books.

There was a loud knock at the door.

"Who is it?" Shuichi asked, opening the door. It was Maiko. "Crap, Sis, it's the middle of the night."

She grimaced. "Is that any way to greet someone doing you a favor? I'm not gonna let you have this now." Maiko pulled something out of her bag and waved it in front of his face. It was the photo album for which he'd been hunting.

"Ooh!" Shuichi grabbed it.

"You said you needed it, right?"

"I love you!" Shuichi tried to throw his arms around her, but Maiko stopped him with a thrust of her hand.

"Gimme some of Yuki's stuff."

"No!" Shuichi cried. "He's all mine! You don't get *anything,* not even a thin little hair from his head!"

"Then you can't have it." Maiko snatched the album out of Shuichi's hands and jammed it back into her bag.

"Maiko! Don't be such a brat!"

She turned her back on him. "Nothing in life is free, Shuichi."

"But that's *already mine!*"

"Got anything to drink?" she asked, ignoring his outburst. She calmly stepped into the kitchen and opened the fridge. She froze for a moment, then let out a bloodcurdling scream.

"There's an alien life form growing in here!"

She grabbed a pair of chopsticks from the counter and used them carefully to remove the offending item. It was unrecognizable, oozing with juice and fuzzy with mold; it could have been anything from a cucumber to a steak, but it was definitely months old.

"I, uh, haven't really been home for a long time."

"You and Yuki too busy with . . . ?" Maiko smiled and looked knowingly at him, but Shuichi ducked his head. He slumped down in the corner and began drawing circles on the wall with his finger.

"What? You two have a fight?" she asked.

"Nope," Shuichi said, looking morose. "I just . . . I remembered that I'm not the only one who loves him."

It wasn't just Maiko who worshipped Yuki. The romance writer had thousands upon thousands of fans in every part of the country. Not only that, but he'd dated a lot of different girls.

Shuichi knew he wasn't the only one aiming for Yuki's heart. *And maybe Yuki doesn't love me. Maybe he just uses me for sex! When I asked him if he hated me, he said the question was stupid.*

"Cheer up! You've got to be strong for Hiro."

"What—why?"

"His mom came by our house last night. Probably 'cause she saw the article in the magazine. She was crazy. She was all like, 'He was such a good studious boy 'til he met that Shuichi of yours and joined that silly band. Now he never listens!' "

So it's true! Where there's smoke, there's fire. Shuichi hugged his knees into his chest and started rocking back and forth. *There's at least some weight to the article. It's not all simply in the past.*

Shuichi thought Hiro had seemed a little different. *All that talk about how being needed made him feel stronger—that was because his mother was nagging him.*

When Shuichi had visited Hiro's house around graduation, his mother had made no attempt to hide the fact that she loathed him.

"Hiro's mom hates me."

"Yup. She was all, 'I don't want that boy to *ruin* my child! I won't let him *corrupt* my Hiro!' And like, she was foaming at the mouth!"

Shuichi put his head in his hands, curling himself into a small ball.

Maiko slapped him jovially on the back. "But Mom's reply was a masterpiece! She kicked Hiro's mom out, shouting things like 'My boy's not a bad influence. It's not like he's a homosexual!' Man, if she only knew you were seeing Eiri Yuki, she'd die! You know, you're a real man-killer!"

Shuichi cried, "What?!"

"You got Nakano to rebel against his parents and leave home. You turned a super-straight stud like Yuki into your lover! *Everyone* falls in love with you." She laughed brightly. "Come on! Stop being all angsty!"

Despite her best efforts, Shuichi was just sinking deeper into depression. Gazing blankly into space, he whispered, "Unrequited love is the most painful thing."

"What're you *talking* about! You're *living* together!"

"You don't get it . . ."

"Shuichi?" Maiko couldn't figure out what was making her brother so mopey. Everything she did just seemed to make things worse, and it was starting to take its toll on her.

Shuichi sighed. *If I keep up like this, I'll depress her too. I can't cause any more trouble for the people around me.* He leapt up abruptly and grabbed the album from his sister.

"Aha! My plan to lower your defenses has succeeded! Thanks, Maiko!"

"You dirty, low down . . . ! Pretending to be depressed!" She huffed. "Whatever, I'll just get something of Yuki's next time. Just you wait!" Maiko stalked out of the apartment, fuming but also relieved that Shuichi wasn't really down.

The moment the door closed behind her, Shuichi rolled back up into a ball on the floor. When he'd said unrequited love, he had meant the sharp contrast in the intensity of feeling between Yuki and himself.

It's so painful when your feelings don't match those of your partner. Even though you're together, you can't be happy because being with him reminds you of how far apart your feelings are.

Yuki doesn't really think of me as his true love, and Hiro's my friend, but he didn't even tell me about his problems.

Shuichi's struggle was also evident in his music. When Shuichi had sung with Ryuichi Sakuma, he had felt a huge gap between their skill levels.

Everything he held most dear seemed to be in danger. Like something was going to snatch his dear ones and his dreams away. No matter how much he loved all of them, and no matter what he did, everything led to suffering. He wanted so much to be needed. It might have been easier if he didn't have to face the people he cared about.

"Isn't it enough just to love them from afar?"

No! My feelings alone can't make any difference. They would all probably be happier if they never knew me.

N-G Pro's publicity department had arranged for Ask to be interviewed for a magazine feature story.

"Sorry it's taking so long," the journalist conducting the interview said. "But it should be a good article. Thank you."

"Don't worry about it. We made you wait while we finished up in the studio." Ask's lead singer, Taki Aizawa, flashed a bright, salesman's smile.

The journalist was writing a puff piece for an idol magazine, so the questions were only the kind of stuff that hardcore fans would find interesting: What was their favorite color? What type of girl did they like? What would they do on a first date? Although the members of Ask considered themselves artists rather than idols, they were professional and polite during the interview. They answered the questions carefully with what they thought girls would want to hear.

"Bad Luck's been having trouble recently," the interviewer said. "Is it true their guitarist is quitting?"

"Bad Luck?" Taki's eyebrow twitched.

"They opened for you once. They're also signed with N-G Pro, right? So I thought you might be friends."

Ma and Ken, Ask's musicians, had been watching the conversation nervously. Now they stepped in.

"I've heard nothing about it at N-G Pro," Ken said.

"We barely see each other, really," Ma added.

"To tell you the truth, I'm worried about them," Taki said, sighing deeply.

The interviewer's smile broadened. Ken and Ma slumped back on the couch.

"I saw him making a phone call to his house from the studio today. You know, they almost split up once before, but I guess the lead singer, what's his name? Shuichi? I guess he insisted he wouldn't sing for any guitarist other than that Nakano guy. You know, I can relate. The three of us have been together from the start, and losing any one of us is unthinkable. It must be really hard for them right now . . ." Taki trailed off, acting sympathetic and looking down at the floor. Suddenly, he looked up again. "Can we take that last bit off the record?" he asked.

"Sure, sure. Off the record."

The interviewer left the meeting very satisfied, and Taki's false concern relieved Ma and Ken.

"For a second, I thought you were gonna pounce on him. Looks like you've finally grown up!" Ma said, brushing back his bangs.

"Yeah, I mean, you've been kinda fixated on them. We were getting a little worried," Ken said, giving Taki a friendly smile and adjusting his sunglasses.

"Fixated?" Taki said sharply. "Why would I be fixated on a band like *that*? They don't even deserve to breathe the same *air* as me, let alone take up my thoughts."

Ma and Ken looked at each other, both thinking the same thing. Taki was still obsessed. But they didn't say anything. They'd been with him for so long, they knew how complicated he was and how dangerous it could be to provoke him.

"All right then." Taki pulled a laptop and a cell phone out of his bag.

"Porn?" Ken asked eagerly, quickly inching closer to the screen in hopes of joining the fun.

"Be careful giving your credit card number to those sites," Ma said, starting to change into his street clothes. "I got ripped off three times."

"Get your minds out of the gutter! I'm not looking at porn!" Taki logged onto the Internet. The website he went to was a forum for music fans, one that had naturally become filled with fans of N-G Pro artists. It acted as a sort of unofficial fan site. Taki had been posting on it under a pseudonym for the last few days.

"I'll use both the press *and* the fans," he murmured, unable to hide a devilish grin.

He had spent a lot of time collecting information from genuine Bad Luck fans, adding rumors that he'd overheard at the office, and embellishing it all to make his posts more effective.

"They're insignificant bugs, but, still . . ."

To Taki, Bad Luck's existence was unbearable. His face contorted into an ugly expression of scorn and fury as his fingers tapped quickly across the keyboard. He smiled, knowing the words he typed would take on a life of their own once they were out in cyberspace.

Track Three:
Irresistible Gravitation

Shuichi stood in front of Yuki's house, clutching the photo album his sister had brought him. He stroked his chin and chuckled to himself. "So my suspicions are confirmed."

Earlier, Yuki had kicked him out of the house for insisting that they look at the album together. When Yuki had refused, Shuichi had whined about it incessantly.

"He doesn't love me," Shuichi said melodramatically. "I know that now. It's all too clear. There's *nothing* left for me here." Although his speech had started as a joke, his eyes filled with tears when he realized that there might be some truth in his words. He stood there with his shoulders hunched over, feeling dejected.

"Yo, Shuichi, my brother picking on you again?" The voice sounded a lot like Yuki's, only it was much more casual. Shuichi spun around.

"Tatsuha!"

The man standing there was Tatsuha Uesugi, Yuki's younger brother. He was Yuki's spitting image, except for his dark hair and black eyes; when they stood together, it was like looking at a yin and yang symbol. It was Tatsuha who had told Shuichi, after Shuichi had known Yuki for months, that "Yuki" was just a penname, and that the writer's real name was Eiri Uesugi.

Tatsuha was a priest. He had a patient, benevolent aura that Shuichi usually responded to by acting like a spoiled, attention-hungry child.

"He doesn't love me!" Shuichi cried, throwing his arms around Tatsuha—who, of course, received him warmly. *If even just a fragment of his kindness could rub off on Yuki, my life would be perfect.* But as much as he liked this gentle priest, Shuichi wasn't in love with Tatsuha. For better or for worse, the one he loved was cold, handsome, unreachable Yuki.

As his face smooshed against Tatsuha's broad chest, Shuichi felt the priest's arms tighten around him. He sensed danger and looked up quickly. A strange glimmer shone in Tatsuha's eyes.

"I want to eat you right up, Ryuichi!" Tatsuha said.

"Whoa! I'm *not* Ryuichi Sakuma! I'm *Shuichi,*" he shouted, trying to get away by thrashing his arms. But Tatsuha wouldn't let him go. "I'm Shuichi Shindou! Your brother's lover!"

Shuichi knew that Tatsuha was in love with Ryuichi. Since Shuichi was an equally petit lead singer in a band with an equally dramatic and uncontrollable personality, Tatsuha often transferred his unrequited love onto Shuichi.

"Yuki's fighting a deadline and has locked himself in the study. He kicked me out of the house. I know you came all the way from Kyoto, but I don't think he'll let you in either."

"You just love to sulk, huh?" Tatsuha patted Shuichi's head. "I couldn't care less if he's here or not."

Shuichi blinked. "What?"

"I came to see you."

"Me?"

"Yeah. I wanted to . . . to ask you for a favor." Uncharacteristically reluctant, Tatsuha began twiddling his thumbs. "It's about Ryuichi . . ."

Shuichi's heartbeat sped up. *Oh no!* The horror of their previous encounters came rushing back to Shuichi. Based solely on their physical resemblance, Tatsuha was going to beg him to replace Ryuichi and do . . . stuff . . . No! *No!*

"Absolutely not!" Shuichi screamed. *It's all your fault, Yuki. You threw me to the wolves, and I hope you suffer endless regret for whatever your brother does to me.*

"Relax!" Tatsuha slapped him in the face to calm him down, but Shuichi was such a lightweight that he fell flat on his back.

"That's what Yuki always says! And you hit me just like he does!" Shuichi remarked as

Tatsuha helped him stand up. "It must run in the family."

"Listen, I want you to . . ." Tatsuha hesitated, still holding onto Shuichi, who was trembling with fear. "I want you to introduce me to Ryuichi!"

Oh, that's all . . . Shuichi came to his senses at last and chuckled sympathetically. "You know, it's not like I ever get to see him either."

"Come on! Just take me backstage with you at your next concert."

"Concert?"

"Yeah, you know, 'Fly to the Next Century,' the music festival."

"Oh, right. Ryuichi mentioned that. Tickets got sold out in like two hours."

"Yeah, that one. It's been so long since Nittle Grasper played live! I got me a ticket, baby! Wait for me, Ryuichi. I'm coming to get you!" Tatsuha nearly exploded into flames of passion.

"Lucky you," Shuichi grumbled. The first time he'd met Tatsuha, they'd spent all night talking about Ryuichi. But now, Shuichi could no longer lose himself so easily just by thinking about his idol. It had once been enough to crush on Ryuichi—and to love Hiro, and music—but now that he had Yuki, he knew that there was so much more to life than just fantasies.

"Well," Tatsuha said, "Ask's playing, so I figured you must be too."

"What?" Shuichi felt blindsided. "I don't . . . I haven't heard anything about it."

N-G Pro had been unusually busy recently, and now that Shuichi thought about it, he had heard that it was because of the music festival. *But why weren't we invited to play?*

"I guess we really have become a variety act." Shuichi's lips twisted into a self-effacing smile. It felt like his ribcage was squeezing all his organs together.

It's not fair. We've been singing, dancing, and joking around like clowns for publicity, because that's what N-G Pro asked us to do. But how can they keep us from performing in their big concert?

Shuichi put his head in his hands and wriggled around in emotional agony.

Meanwhile, Tatsuha was lost in his daydream. "Ryuichi, you're even cuter in the flesh. My hands and lips will show you the way to heaven!" Tatsuha became even more worked up, eventually using R-rated words to describe his plans for Nittle Grasper's singer.

But Shuichi wasn't paying attention. There was just too much happening at once. Yesterday, Yuki had rejected him. Today, he found out Hiro's mother was still against their music career. Maybe if Bad Luck hit the top of the charts and sold millions of records, then Hiro's mother would be forced to change her mind. But now, instead of being given a chance, Bad Luck was being denied a major opportunity.

"Tell me it's not true! Please, tell me it's not true!" Shuichi sobbed.

"I love you, Ryuichi!" Tatsuha sobbed louder.

Both men screamed at the top of their lungs, then they stopped abruptly. Each looked at the other as the same thought dawned on them at the exact same time.

"You said Yuki's got a deadline?" Tatsuha asked.

"Yeah, he already kicked me out."

They both gulped, fearing that they might have already disturbed the writer.

"Let's go somewhere else and talk, okay?" Shuichi suggested.

"Good idea."

They nodded at each other, but it was too late. Shuichi turned slowly. The door was half open, and Yuki, whose beautiful face was marred by the effects of his all-nighter, glared daggers at them.

"A wise decision."

Shuichi was sure he saw an inhuman, maniacal gloss in those big brown eyes. Had it taken them even a second longer to notice Yuki standing there, it was very possible they'd both be dead.

Shuichi and Tatsuha got drinks from a vending machine and then sat down on a park bench.

"A toast to our bad luck!" cried Tatsuha. They tapped their cans together.

"It's all my fault," Shuichi muttered into his oolong tea. "I'm just not good enough."

"Tell me about it. If you were in that music festival, you'd be all happy, and I could meet my Ryuichi."

"At least you still get to watch the concert." Shuichi pouted.

"You can too."

"Nah," Shuichi said. "I don't . . . I mean, sure, I wanna hear Nittle Grasper play, but . . ." Listening wasn't enough. Shuichi wanted to share the stage with them.

He had always thought that Ryuichi was a genius, but his feelings had intensified since Bad Luck's debut concert, when Ryuichi had saved him from embarrassment. Sure, they'd sung together that day, but it had been spontaneous. Shuichi had not been prepared. He wanted to do it *right*.

Shuichi gazed up at the flickering streetlights. This was the same park where he had first met Yuki. Shuichi was so happy that he'd somehow managed to make Yuki his lover. *But is Yuki really happy? Maybe I've made everything worse. Maybe*

I've just caused him more headaches. And I've made Hiro fight with his mother again—without even realizing it. Maybe I'm just a problem for everybody after all.

"I thought loving Yuki was a good thing," Shuichi murmured. "Sure, going around, shouting 'I love you' and flinging myself all over him got me what I wanted, but now that I look back, I was also so caught up in my own desires that I didn't even realize I was making trouble for everyone around me."

And I don't think I've really accomplished a single thing by myself. Hiro is the only reason we were signed, and Hiro was always there for me when I had problems with Yuki. But I've never done anything for him!

"And Yuki!" Shuichi shouted out. "Yuki let me be his lover because I was persistent, but have I ever helped him with anything? I bug him, and I keep him from finishing his novels on time! I'm just a parasite!"

"My brother's not exactly a philanthropist," Tatsuha said. "He wouldn't be with someone he didn't like."

"But I want him to *love* me. I want him to be all *mine.*"

I thought love was supposed to be a thing of beauty. But it turns out I'm just selfish and greedy. Shuichi slumped over.

"You sure fell for a tricky one," Tatsuha said, mussing Shuichi's hair. "But don't give up on Yuki."

Tatsuha's kindness was astonishing. *How could anyone be so nice to his brother's lover?*

"When an apple falls," Tatsuha continued, "it's pulled toward the earth, but the apple is also pulling the *earth* toward *it.*"

"It is? How?" Shuichi asked with genuine curiosity. "That's amazing! Every time something falls, the earth moves too?"

Shuichi looked so completely baffled that Tatsuha glared at him with irritation.

"Um, you *did* go to high school, right? How come you don't know the basics of physics?"

"I got, like, straight D's," Shuichi said, suddenly happy. "If Hiro hadn't let me copy his work, I wouldn't have graduated!"

"Aha! That explains it," Tatsuha said. "Okay, so the earth's too big to move in any way we can measure, but it's moving, yes."

"Dude, really?"

"So, it's like, the apple's plunging straight toward the earth, and the earth reflexively spins, like it's automatically moving forward to catch it."

"But how?"

"If I go any further, you'll have to make an offering to the temple," Tatsuha said. "This is sermon territory."

"I don't even get what you're talking about." Shuichi frowned.

Tatsuha nodded. "But that very quality might be your saving grace."

"What?" Shuichi looked up at him, wide-eyed. He squirmed like a happy puppy, wagging his tail. "How?"

Shuichi's reaction made Tatsuha want to tease him. "You could ask Yuki to clear it up for you."

"I hate you!" Shuichi turned his back on Tatsuha. "I should've never brought it up." His earlier sadness was now completely drowned out by anger.

If this were Ryuichi, Tatsuha thought to himself, *I would throw him to the ground right here, right now, and have my way with him.*

"My brother must love having you around." *A lovable idiot,* Tatsuha thought, *with no complications—direct, honest, and defenseless. Yet he has the power to rip reactions right out of you.* "Take care of him, Shuichi."

Tatsuha smiled slightly, looking just like his brother.

The next morning, Shuichi was in good spirits when he left his apartment and headed to the TV studio where *Sing! Dance! Bonbaban!* was being filmed. Tatsuha had spent the night in Shuichi's apartment, but he had already left.

"It's a shame nothing happened last night," Tatsuha had joked as he left. "But thanks for letting me crash here. I'll be sure to show

my gratitude to you some time." He winked
playfully.

Chills ran up Shuichi's spine. He knew it was
dangerous to let Tatsuha stay with him, but there
was nothing Shuichi could do. Yuki wasn't going
to let his brother in, and sleeping in the park at
this time of year was basically suicide.

Shuichi was overcome with longing at the
thought of Yuki, but he couldn't bother the older
man now. Yuki would be finished with his writing
at the end of the day, and Shuichi could see him
then. Right now, the only thing Shuichi could do
was throw himself into his own work.

*It might be just a variety show, but if the
audience has a good time, they'll remember my name
and face. If enough people do that, Bad Luck might
have a chance to be included in the New Year's
concert. And who knows, maybe we can convince
Hiro's mother to support us.*

"I'm coming, *Sing! Dance! Bonbaban!* And
I'm gonna blow you away!"

Shuichi was about to fling open the waiting
room door, when K appeared out of nowhere

and knocked him down. Shuichi flopped on the floor like a fish and somehow landed safely across the room. "How am I supposed to do this show wounded?" he raged. "Some manager you are!"

"A manager's job is to protect his clients." Gun in hand, K kicked open the door and went about inspecting every nook and cranny of the room.

"Um . . . K?"

"Danger! Stay back!"

A passerby might have found K's one-man action movie hilarious, but the blond took himself so seriously that Shuichi obeyed without protest. Forced to wait, Shuichi drifted to the couch where Suguru and Sakano were talking.

"Tohma said *that?*"

"His exact words were 'if it crushes them, then that's all they were worth,' " Suguru said. "You're the producer. I think you should talk to him, or ask Tohma to. Make sure he's okay, make sure his head's in the game."

They must be talking about Hiro, Shuichi thought. He instantly drew back into the shadows and eavesdropped.

"I don't mean to sound harsh," Sakano said. "But the president does have a point."

"I know," Suguru said. "Tohma understands the industry inside and out. I'm sure he's right. But I still have my doubts. I mean, even Ask gets to play at the festival."

"Tohma has his reasons." Sakano sighed. "That website has been getting worse. Detailed schedules, fragments of conversations . . . it seems like an old fan is somehow getting into places he really shouldn't be. He may even be stalking the band."

"So that's why K's dissecting the waiting room? I thought he'd just gone crazy."

Shuichi couldn't help but feel guilty. *I'm sorry I ever let you get on my nerves, Suguru. You really are part of this band. You're really trying to do what's best for us.*

Shuichi felt so emotional that he wanted to take his feelings, put them in a song, and sing them for everyone watching the show that night.

If we ever get a chance to do a concert or a music program, we'll grab it and make it ours. Right, Hiro? And then everyone will know who we are!

Shuichi felt even more revved up than usual as these thoughts ran through his mind.

"Sing! Dance! Bonbaban!" the announcer said. "Today's guests are the comic trio The Three Thorns, and Bad Luck!"

On cue, the three members of Bad Luck stepped out onto the stage, smiling brightly.

"Judging from that intro," Hiro sighed, smiling, "Bad Luck is a comic trio as well."

"Why can't they introduce us as musicians and mention that our single is selling well?" Suguru whispered.

Shuichi didn't care. He was in his element. The bright lights and the hundreds of faces in the crowd filled him with energy. "Don't get hung up on that. It's live television. Let's kick butt, so everyone watching will remember us."

Sing! Dance! Bonbaban! consisted of several physical challenges interspersed with conversations with the host. If a team could skillfully manipulate

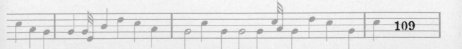

the flow of a conversation and bring a song into play, they'd earn extra points. Each team was only allowed to sing five previously selected songs, so you had to wrest the conversation away from the other team.

Bad Luck happened to be the first real band to appear on the show. The show's producers probably didn't even *know* that they were a band.

"And now, let's play Once Upon a Time!"

This event involved childhood photographs of both teams' members. The pictures were lined up like a game of solitaire. If you managed to line up all three pictures from your team, you won the game. But to get a picture, you had to risk life and limb. The contestants had to stick their heads into a barrel of flour and come out with a small piece of candy held between their teeth.

"I'm first!" Shuichi shouted.

"No, Shuichi! You're our singer!" Suguru cried, grabbing Shuichi's arm. "You can't sing with a face covered in flour!"

Hiro stepped up to the barrel. He looked over at Shuichi, took a deep breath, and, with what appeared to be a surge of power, dunked his head into the flour. He writhed around, half-submerged, and when he finally rose, his long hair had turned white, he had a piece of red candy wedged between his front teeth.

Hiro, you've done it! You've won the first round for Bad Luck!

Hiro was given the picture he'd been playing for—a snapshot of himself at his high school graduation. The master of ceremonies quickly turned to the subject of Hiro's entrance exams.

"Bad Luck's guitarist, Hiroshi Nakano! Recently, there have been rumors you're planning to enter med school."

"Speaking of studying," one of the Three Thorns interjected, trying to steal the spotlight. But the MC ignored the interruption and thrust a microphone into Hiro's face, eager to get the scoop on all the recent gossip involving Bad Luck.

"Is there any truth to the rumors? Because from what I gather, you've always had very high grades."

"Nah, I spent most of the time playing with him," Hiro said, pointing at Shuichi.

Shuichi grabbed the mic and kicked into high gear. "We used to pretend to be Nittle Grasper!" And without warning, he started to sing his favorite song, "Be There."

The next game was Wasabi Russian Roulette. One contestant had to spin a giant roulette wheel, and if he landed on the wrong number, he'd be forced to eat a giant piece of sushi that had an ice-cream scoop's worth of wasabi on it.

"Tuna sushi . . ." Shuichi drooled, but once again was stopped by his teammates.

"What if you lose?" Hiro asked. "You won't be able to sing with your mouth burning from the wasabi!"

"Well, *I* can't go," Suguru said. "Wasabi's way too spicy for me!"

"Oh," Shuichi said. "I forgot that Suguru's a wimp when it comes to food. Go get 'em, Hiro!"

"All right!"

Hiro spun the wheel and won again. This time, he came back with a picture of Suguru as a baby, cradled in Tohma's arms.

"Bad Luck's keyboardist, Suguru Fujisaki, is the cousin of Tohma Seguchi of Nittle Grasper fame!" the MC announced. "Genius must be genetic!"

"Uh . . . I . . ." Suguru froze up, so Shuichi stole the mic again.

"Suguru's talent is due solely to his hard work! To prove it, I'm gonna sing a song he arranged!" And once again, Shuichi started passionately singing one of their songs, using every ounce of energy he had to give.

His powerful voice made the audience and crew forget for a moment that this was a variety show. They had been laughing at him a moment before, but now they looked on in rapture. They had fallen in love with his voice.

"Wow!" the MC said after Shuichi was done. "Guess you boys are real musicians."

Hearing this, Hiro and Suguru gave Shuichi congratulatory thumbs up. Shuichi beamed, even more revved up than before.

It was time for the last contest, which was always the craziest. Today's event made the audience gasp—The Eel Bath.

That was all that had been in the script, so they had all assumed there would be a tank of water with an eel or two, and someone would have to reach in and pull one out. But the tank that entered the studio contained *only* eels—hundreds of them.

"Eek!" Suguru squealed like a little girl. Just looking at it made his skin crawl.

"Well, well, this is certainly something," the MC said. "The first person to swim through this is the winner."

The leader of the Three Thorns took to the start platform, sporting a tragic expression.

"On your mark. Get set. Go!"

The words were barely out of his mouth when Shuichi dove into the tank. He seemed happy as he parted the eels before him. He made his way through the tank fearlessly, compelled by a mysterious, unstoppable force. When he reached the end, Shuichi jumped out to retrieve his own photograph.

With all three photographs, Bad Luck had won the game. Smiling and laughing, Shuichi

pulled an eel out of his shirt and waved it around.

"I'll bring this one home for dinner, Mom!"

"Well, that kind of energy and teamwork should put a stop to those rumors that you're breaking up!" the MC said enthusiastically. "If you quit, the world would truly lose some gifted comedians!"

"We're a *band!*" Shuichi snapped.

The lights went down and the show's credits rolled across the monitors.

Despite being called comedians, Shuichi felt intensely satisfied. *I sang well, the audience had a great time, and we won. Even Hiro's mother must have changed her mind.*

As Shuichi made his way out of the station, he noticed a woman standing just outside the exit. He recognized her immediately and waved innocently.

"Hi there. Did you see the show?" he asked.

"Yes. We need to talk. Do you mind?" she asked anxiously.

"Oh, um . . . okay," Shuichi said, figuring she wanted to talk about the show. "Hiro'll be out as soon as his hair dries."

"No, I want to talk to *you*. Alone."

She grabbed Shuichi's hand just as Suguru walked out of the backstage door. "What's up, Shuichi? Who's—"

"Suguru, we're done working, right?" Shuichi called over his shoulder.

"Yeah." Suguru blinked, confused.

"Okay then. Bye," Shuichi said, stepping into a taxi with the middle-aged woman.

"Shuichi! What's going on? Should I get the manager?"

"Nah, this is Hiro's mom!" Shuichi smiled brightly.

The taxi took off, leaving Suguru staring blankly after it.

The backstage door creaked open. "Sorry to keep you waiting, man. This long hair takes forever to dry." Hiro ran his fingers through his damp hair.

"Where's Shuichi? Did he leave already? Desperate to see Yuki again?" he chuckled.

"No . . . he, uh . . . went off with your mom."

"What?" Hiro's expression froze. "Was she mad? Was she screaming?"

"No. She acted just like you, relaxed and smiling."

"Uh-oh." Hiro blanched.

"Is there a problem?"

"She only smiles when she's enraged." Hiro bit his lip. "Her beef is with me. What's she want with Shuichi?"

Meanwhile, in the N-G Pro building, Ryuichi and Tohma had just finished watching *Sing! Dance! Bonbaban!* in Tohma's office.

"Shuichi is really a good singer." Ryuichi Sakuma thrust a stuffed bunny named Kumaguro into Tohma's face and wiggled it about, as if it was doing the talking. "Isn't he, Tohma?" (There were very few people who could get away with treating the president of N-G Pro like that.) "But I think *I* should be the one to sing *my* song."

"You'll get to sing at the festival, Ryuichi," Tohma said, trying to placate him.

"Oh, yeah. I hope I can sing with Shuichi again."

"With Shuichi?" Tohma frowned. "You don't want to sing with Nittle Grasper?"

Ryuichi revised his statement quickly. "I didn't mean at the same time. I like listening to his songs, too."

Tohma peered at him. "You like his voice that much?"

"Yes!" Ryuichi replied with a smile so sweet and ingenuous that it could awaken the maternal instinct even in a man.

"Hm." Tohma thought for a moment. Then he smiled. "Why don't we do it?"

"Hooray! I did it, Kumagoro!" Ryuichi said to his stuffed bunny. "I can sing with Shuichi!" He began running around the office. "Shuichi and me in the festival together!" His voice was so loud and vibrant that it passed through the wall and reached Taki, who was eavesdropping in the next room.

"He's going to be in the music festival? On the same stage as *me?*" Taki's shoulders shook with fury. "Why him? Why is it always him?!"

First they give him a brilliant manager, the same one who made Ryuichi a hit in America. Then they sign Tohma Seguchi's little prodigy on as their keyboardist. And now this!

Even though he had leaked the story about Hiro to the press, and even though he had put the rumors on the Internet, Bad Luck was doing better than ever.

"He'll *never* share a stage with *me!*" Taki whispered cruelly.

Track Four:
Unacceptable Feelings

"Hiro's room hasn't changed at all," Shuichi said as he walked through the Nakano residence. Hiro's mother had brought him there directly after the show.

The two boys had played in that house since elementary school. After they'd formed their band, they often practiced right in this very room. They had done their homework together at that table, or, to be more exact, Hiro had done his homework and Shuichi had copied it. They had stayed up late so many nights in Hiro's room, talking endlessly about music, and dreaming of their future together.

Shuichi flipped through a few of the textbooks piled high on the desk, and it felt like he had been transported back in time.

"I've kept everything exactly as it was when Hiroshi left the house," Mrs. Nakano said coldly. "Ready for him to get back to studying."

"But you saw us on TV . . ." He had thought their performance on the show had convinced her to support Hiro. He had assumed she'd brought him here because she wanted to apologize.

Shuichi put the textbook back on the stack and turned around to look at her. Now he saw how wrong he'd been; she had a faint smile on her face, but her eyes burned with fury.

"Oh, yes. I saw you on that insipid TV show. *That* was the last straw. I will never again stand idly by and watch Hiro make a spectacle of himself in front of the entire country. He will quit your little group this very day."

Oh, no, Shuichi thought. *All our efforts have backfired.*

Everyone in the audience had enjoyed the silly games they had played. It had been a successful day, Shuichi thought, because they had convinced a lot of people that Bad Luck was not only funny, but also talented.

"Why?" Shuichi asked quietly.

"No decent parent would stand by and let their child become a laughingstock!"

"Really?" Shuichi's family had watched him do silly things on TV before, and they had always laughed. They knew he was going to be even more ridiculous than usual when he appeared on *Sing! Dance! Bonbaban!* and they'd been looking forward to it. They'd even promised to record it.

"I understand," Shuichi said, trying to be tactful even though he had no idea what she meant.

"Good. If you accept this, then Hiroshi will . . ."

"I will never let Hiroshi be unhappy!" Shuichi cried, dropping suddenly to his knees. "I'll make sure our next release sells a million copies!"

"A million?" Mrs. Nakano spat out. "You're dreaming."

"Then I'll play on the street corner. I'll make sure Hiro will never go hungry as long as we're together!"

"You can suit yourself, but don't you dare drag my beautiful child into your silly fantasies!" she screamed.

Shuichi thought back to when he'd been a boy. Hiro's mother had smiled and laughed when they'd first sang for her. She had not objected at all when they started their band. It was only during high school, when it came time to talk about college and the future, that she started to object. For her, dreams were useless; happiness was useless. She thought that earning a lot of money by working in a respectable profession was the only path to a fulfilling life.

"Please tell Hiro he doesn't have to quit music!" Shuichi bowed his head respectfully.

"Stop that groveling. If groveling were any use, I'd do it myself! Anything to save my son."

Shuichi flung his arms around her legs desperately. "Hiro said all he wants is to play music with me! That's what makes him happy! Being with me makes him happy."

Mrs. Nakano misinterpreted Shuichi's words and the love she saw in his eyes to suggest something other than what Shuichi had meant.

"He would never say something like that! You put him up to it!" She began kicking her legs, trying to get rid of him. "You've changed him. His brother Yuji is wasting his life trying to be an actor, but Hiroshi had a future! He was my only hope! What have you done to him?"

"Done? Hey, I didn't do anything to him!" Shuichi wailed.

"Liar! It's twisted. You're sick. If only he could be hung up over a girl instead!"

"What?" Surprised, Shuichi let go of her legs in surprise, just as she was trying to break free. She accidentally kicked him right in the face.

He was used to Yuki kicking him, so the blow itself wasn't so bad, but he was still reeling from what she had said, so he ended up crumpled in a heap.

"Ah!" Hiro's mom recovered her senses and scurried to his side. "Oh my, I didn't mean to hurt you. I'm sorry, but you suddenly let go."

Shuichi looked pale. "I . . . Hiro and I . . ."

She blanched. "You didn't really have . . . with my son." She slumped against the wall, unable to go on.

"No, no! Nothing like that!" Shuichi frantically tried to clear things up. He couldn't deny the fact that he had hooked up with another man, but Hiro was straight. He had been with plenty of girls in high school. Shuichi loved him, of course, but in a brotherly way.

"Listen—no guitar, no band, no artistic dreams. That boy will be a doctor." She glared down at Shuichi. "He doesn't listen to me, but he listens to you."

"But I . . ." Shuichi didn't know what to say.

Mrs. Nakano interpreted his silence as agreement. Her expression relaxed.

"All right, good. Well, I am sorry that I dragged you here and screamed at you," she said, shoving him toward the door. "Shuichi, you should rethink things as well. You simply can't make a living as an artist or a musician, even if you love it."

"I know," he said politely, despite having been insulted and abused. "Thank you." Shuichi left the Nakano residence and wandered aimlessly down the familiar streets.

She had been crazy at first, he thought, but deep down, Hiro's mom was still the same nice lady that had given them snacks when he came to visit. When she kicked him, she had been genuinely concerned. *She's just overcome with worry.*

"But why isn't it enough for him to love music? What gives her the right to decide his future for him? She should understand that he just doesn't want to be a doctor."

Is it really that bad that Hiro loves music? That he wants to make a living from it? And is it really that bad that a man could love another man? That I love Yuki?

He remembered Mrs. Nakano's violent disgust, and his heart sank. *Are my feelings so unacceptable?*

Shuichi kept walking, completely unaware of where he was going. He crossed the street, and although he was almost run over by a speeding car, he didn't notice it.

"I wouldn't be able to go on living if someone told me I couldn't play music or love Yuki." For Shuichi, loving music and loving Yuki were feelings he couldn't ignore. They were as essential to his everyday life as eating and breathing.

"But maybe Yuki would be happier if I didn't love him . . ." *I want to see him, but all I ever do is make Yuki angry. All I do is interfere with his work.*

Shuichi knew he couldn't go back to Yuki's house. He wandered on, crossing a wide boulevard, but still paying no attention to where his feet took him.

"Yo, Shuichi, what're you doing here?" It was his sister's voice. He suddenly noticed that he was standing in front of his parents' house. He had unconsciously followed his old route home from Hiro's house.

"Maiko!"

"Are you returning the album?" she asked.

"Um, no."

"I saw you on TV. You're an idiot, you know? Mom and Dad just about peed their pants, they were laughing so hard." Maiko dragged him inside. "Mom! Shuichi's come home!"

His mother emerged from the kitchen, wiping her hands on her apron. "Well, this is a surprise. You bring us that eel?"

"No, they said they were saving them for a different show." Shuichi shrugged.

"You come home unannounced like this . . . I don't have enough for dinner. I'll have to buy more," she grumbled affectionately. She left the house abruptly.

"Is she angry?" Shuichi asked. But his concern was unnecessary. She came back in under ten minutes with *yakiniku* ingredients, and set about making a feast for her long-absent son.

"I'm sure all you eat is junk," Shuichi's mother said as they sat down to eat. "Maiko told me you hardly ever use your kitchen, that your fridge is filled with rotting vegetables. Piles of garbage. Typical! Men just can't live by themselves."

Shuichi squirmed. "Well, I . . ."

"You ought to get yourself a nice girlfriend to cook for you."

"Uh . . ." Shuichi glared at Maiko, who was stifling her laughter.

Yuki lived alone, but he was an excellent cook, and his house was always immaculate. Shuichi had almost told her what a wonderful cook his boyfriend was, that he fed Shuichi nutritious, exotic delicacies every night. But he couldn't quite bring himself to fess up, and instead sat silently, savoring the taste of his mother's *yakiniku*.

"Don't forget your vegetables," his mother said, filling his plate with a second helping.

"You work hard every day. It must take its toll on you," his father remarked, piling more meat on his plate.

"Oh, it's usually not so bad," Shuichi said. He felt keenly just how lucky he was to have this sort of support from his family. But after dinner, when he went up to his old room, his heart wavered.

His bedroom had been transformed into storage. Boxes were everywhere, and there was even a pile of stuff on top of his bed. Shuichi flopped down in a small clearing on the floor. He momentarily doubted his family's love for him, thinking that Hiro was more treasured because his mom had kept his room unchanged. But Shuichi's family had watched *Sing! Dance! Bonbaban!* and they'd laughed. They appreciated their son, unlike Hiro's mother.

Of course, for Shuichi's family, watching him do stupid stuff on TV wasn't very different from real life; when he still lived at home, they were constantly laughing at his antics. They embraced Shuichi just as he was. They accepted that he'd moved on, chosen his own path.

Home, sweet home. Shuichi loved the way his sister and mother fussed over him and how his father just grinned. Here, unlike at Yuki's, he could be himself and not worry about getting on anyone's nerves.

"Then why do I miss his sneer? Is that strange?" he asked aloud, staring up at the ceiling.

Both his body and heart yearned for Yuki. But at the same time, Shuichi was fed up with unrequited affection. *I'm only putting the band's reputation in danger—Hiro's mom just reminded me of how unacceptable my feelings are to the outside world.*

He sighed deeply, just as Maiko came into the room.

"It's changed a lot, huh?"

"It's not my room anymore." He gave a pained smile. The words "my room" didn't even apply to his own apartment these days. His room was at Yuki's house.

"It was fun having you home again," Maiko said, sitting with her back to his.

"Really?" Shuichi asked, blushing.

"Yeah, despite everything, we still miss you."

"Despite what?" cried Shuichi.

Maiko leaned farther back against him. "You leave the house, start living alone, release a CD. Like, millions of people I've never met know who you are. I can't even get to the damn convenience store without hearing your song on the radio."

"Really? That's awesome." Shuichi smiled softly.

"Yeah. But it's like you've gone to some far-off world. I miss you."

"Come on. It's just Hiro and me playing in our band, like always."

"But before, when you did concerts or festivals, I used to help out. Now you're living it up somewhere, and I can't keep up with you." Maiko sounded really sad.

"Living it up?"

"I hope you realize how amazing it is that you can make a living doing what you love!"

Shuichi's spirits sank again. Memories overwhelmed him. He suddenly felt that he couldn't live up to everyone's expectations—he couldn't be a true genius. Bad Luck wasn't even treated like a real band.

He sighed. "I feel like there's not much further we can go, just because we love it."

"But you're just getting started! The sky's the limit!"

He shook his head. "Nope. It's like unrequited love. They aren't even letting us play at the festival."

"Unrequited love? You're an idiot. You know how many people are trying to make it in music? Most of them never even get a CD released."

"I know, but a CD's like standing on the start line."

Stop! This isn't me! I'm not a pessimist. Shuichi leaned all his weight back against his sister.

"My boyfriend told me," Maiko said, "that dogs can tell which people are dog-lovers. Same with people. Someone approaches us with love in their heart, and we open ourselves up to accept them. I think if you keep singing with love, then the God of music will give you his blessings."

"You're crazy," Shuichi said affectionately. "But that does sound nice."

"Beause it's true," she said pushing back on him hard. "Hey, so what's up with your boyfriend?"

"Dunno," he said, toppling over onto the floor. "I've been telling him over and over that I love him, but he's just as cold as ever. I'm starting to think that continuing our relationship might not be possible."

"Why not?"

Shuichi sank even deeper into despair. He looked like he was about to cry.

"Shuichi!" his mother's voice called out from downstairs. "Someone's here to see you!"

For a second, he felt hope. *Yuki's deadline was yesterday, and he might have come to get me . . . but that would never happen. Why am I even thinking it?*

Maiko smiled and left him to his thoughts.

A few seconds later, Hiro stepped into the room. "You ditched me at the station!"

Shuichi had known it would be Hiro, but he cried anyway. He wanted to see Yuki more than anything.

"Sorry about my mom, Shuichi." Hiro handed him a handkerchief.

"It's not that. That's not your fault anyway."

"No," Hiro said in a serious tone. "I should have talked this out with her a long time ago.

Tonight, I'll make her understand that you're more important than anything."

"Oh! A confession of love!" Shuichi cried, waving his hand daintily.

Hiro snorted, scratching his head. "I do feel like the spineless husband trapped in a war between his wife and mother."

"Husband my foot! You may be my best friend, but you can't take the place of Yuki!" Suddenly, Shuichi's heart filled with resolve. *This is no time for fussing and whining! I've only got one place I need to go!*

"Uh . . . Shuichi?" Hiro said, but Shuichi had barreled out of the door and was already out of sight. "Dang, I didn't get a chance to tell him the good news."

K had told Hiro about their next job.

"But before I get into that, I've got to take care of something," he murmured.

He bit his lip.

You may have given birth to me, but I won't tolerate anyone making Shuichi sad. Not even you, Mom.

"You heading for a fight?" Yuji asked in a sunny voice. "You look crazed." He stood in the doorway of their parent's house, his sunglasses pushed up on his head.

"Something like that. All she cares about is appearances," Hiro spat out. "Always throwing around words like *shameful* and *embarrassing*. Only thinking about herself, never about my feelings."

"Of course she's selfish. We all are," Yuji said, nodding sagely. "You know, someday we should do a sitcom together. I'll be the star, and a song of yours can play during the opening credits."

The sudden change of subject made Hiro even madder. "This is no time for dreams!"

"What? What's this? One lousy CD released and you stop dreaming?" Yuji teased.

"Of course not!"

"Then what's the problem? We know where we're going." Yuji's laid-back manner was slowly soothing over Hiro's rage. "I've been looking for day jobs, just to pay the bills, you know? It's hard. Not that many people will let you take time off if you suddenly get an audition."

If his parents had steered the conversation this way, Hiro might have been offended. But it was different coming from his brother.

"You know, you were always their favorite," Yuji said. "They brought you up more carefully than me, but you still turned your back on them. You can't really blame them for being mad about it."

"You're saying I'm ungrateful?" Hiro cried. "I can't let her treat Shuichi like that."

"Oh, Hiro!" their mother cried from the doorway, thrilled to see her son at home. "I knew you'd come back. You were meant for better things!" She took his arm, beckoning him into the house, but he gently shook her off. "Hiro?"

"I love music, Mom. I love playing music with Shuichi. That's what I do." He took an envelope out of his pocket. There was a ticket inside it. "I know you might have gotten the wrong impression from watching the variety show, but if you watch this, I'm sure you'll understand."

Hiro smiled kindly at her, but she just stood there, flabbergasted, as if unable to believe the words coming out of her son's mouth.

"Come and watch us. See how happy I am when we play together."

Shuichi's heart pounded as he stood in front of Yuki's apartment. "I hope he doesn't kick me out again."

He took a deep breath and reached for the door. But before he touched the knob, the door swung open.

"I thought you were never coming home," Yuki complained, but there was also a note of pleasure in his voice. Shuichi took this as a positive sign.

"I'm sorry I was so selfish yesterday," Shuichi said. "Did you finish your work?"

Yuki swept some hair off his face then turned away, as if searching for the right words.

"The book isn't finished yet. And it's all your fault," he spat out.

A small ray of hope shone in Shuichi's heart. "Were you worried because I didn't come back? So worried that you couldn't finish your book?"

Yuki cocked his head. "I hear something talking, but I can't understand such nonsense."

He tried to slam the door, but Shuichi threw his weight against it. "Wait! Can I stay?" He stared at Yuki. "Can I make love to you?"

Yuki blinked. "You ask that now?"

"Now. Of course!" *Some romance novelist.* Shuichi decided he needed to be bold. "If you don't give me a clear answer, I'm gonna have to assume it's a 'yes!' " Shuichi started to push on the door with all his strength. It suddenly fell away, and he tumbled onto the hardwood floor.

"Good enough answer?" Yuki said with a cold but beautiful glare. "Someone like you shouldn't be worried about *my* feelings. You got this far just on your own passion, so why demand answers from me now?" Yuki reached out his hand to help Shuichi up. "Get up and get in here."

"Yuki!" Sobbing tears of joy, Shuichi reached for Yuki's hand, but Yuki snatched it away at the last minute.

Shuichi leapt toward him, throwing his arms around his shoulders. "Aw, you're all embarrassed now."

Yuki dragged his little burden into the house without answering.

"You don't mind that I love you, do you?" Shuichi whispered.

Yuki stayed silent.

"It's no good," Shuichi continued. "No matter what part of me you cut open, all you'll ever find inside is love."

"Let go." Yuki shrugged.

"Nope," Shuichi tightened his grip. *I'll never let go, no matter what you say.* "You never let me touch you, so I'm gonna make the moment last."

Yuki laughed. "I know how you feel."

"Huh?" Shuichi reeled in shock.

Yuki bent close for a kiss. He hesitated at the last moment.

"Yuki?" Shuichi asked breathlessly

The gentle press of Yuki's lips against his own made Shuichi weak in the knees. He slumped against the wall as Yuki pressed in on him. Yuki parted Shuichi's mouth and kissed him deeply, humming softly.

"All the frustration I feel at having blown my deadline?" he whispered in Shuichi's ear. "I'm gonna take it out on you." Yuki thrust his hips forward, grinding against Shuichi, clearly enjoying himself.

"Wah!" Shuichi clutched at Yuki's shoulders.

I guess he's angry about yesterday! I wish I knew if this was about interfering with work, or not coming home. But I don't mind if he bullies me. I don't mind if he teases me. Or even if he gets a little bit rough. As long as we're together, I'm happy.

But still, I do want to hear those three little words. I want him to accept me and to tell me it's okay that I love him.

"Oh," he gasped, as Yuki licked a hot trail down his neck. He panted while Yuki yanked off their clothes.

As Yuki had his way, Shuichi's anxieties melted, dissipating in the friction between their bodies.

"Hey, Shuichi is playing at the festival," Maiko said as she looked at the unofficial Bad Luck fan site where rumors about Hiro had first appeared, and information was still coming in fast. Now the fan forum had revealed that Bad Luck had suddenly been added to the roster for the Fly to the Next Century music festival.

Thank goodness, Maiko thought, as she posted a note on the site expressing her approval. But a very disturbing post appeared right after hers.

"No way! What's up with that?"

It was from "Chita," a so-called fan who had been posting recently. He knew an awful lot about Bad Luck, but was very critical of them. He wasn't happy with the band's newfound success.

The post read, "Let's try and stop Bad Luck from getting to the festival." It also contained the license plate and description of their shuttle van. Messages that objected to Chita's suggestion quickly appeared, but there were also several that agreed.

"This doesn't look good."

Maiko quickly called her brother's cell phone, but it was switched off.

Track Five:
Fly, Bad Luck!

The next morning, just before dawn, a mysterious van pulled up in front of Yuki's house. A tall, blond man emerged from the van and abducted Shuichi at gunpoint. He threw Shuichi into the backseat and then the van sped off, its tires squealing. Inside, Shuichi found the other members and staff of Bad Luck, each looking very grim.

"Um, what's happening? Where are we going?" Shuichi asked, unable to stand the somber silence any longer.

No one answered. K was notorious for not telling them where they were going or what they were doing, but Shuichi had never seen everyone looking as serious as they did now.

What's all this? Somebody please, tell me! There I was, sharing a special moment with Yuki at last, and this crazed Yankee barges in! Sure, after . . . Yuki was done . . . he ignored me and spent all night plugging away at his novel, but I wanted to wake up staring into his beautiful face!

Oh, Yuki!

I know he's got deadlines, but he didn't even come out of his study when his own lover was being kidnapped. He could've at least given me a good-bye kiss.

"I think we might get there intact," Sakano said with relief. He was driving, his face tight with tension.

K sat in the passenger seat beside Sakano. He was armed even more heavily than usual. He actually had an assault rifle. Hiro, laid-back as always, sat next to Shuichi, as did Suguru, who seemed unexpectedly calm. All of their instruments and equipment were stuffed in between their seats.

"Where are we going?" Shuichi whispered.

"The festival," Hiro said. "To play."

"The what? To huh?" Shuichi's mouth gaped open.

"You know, 'Fly to the Next Century,' the music festival," Hiro said patiently.

"The New Year's concert? The one Nittle Grasper's playing at?"

Hiro nodded. "Yup. We heard and were on board just after you left yesterday."

"Amazing!" Shuichi jumped up and down in his seat, making the entire van wobble. "I gotta tell Yuki!"

He whipped out his cell phone. After a moment's pause, Yuki answered. All of Shuichi's previous worries vanished, so he took this as an excuse to be even more needy than usual.

"I know you're working, but we're gonna be playing at the big music festival today. And it'll be live on TV and everything, so you should watch, please. I mean, the video's already set to tape the thing, but . . . please . . ."

Yuki's response wasn't exactly enthusiastic, so Shuichi's voice jumped a few decibels. "Bad

Luck *and* Nittle Grasper! I'm *begging* you to watch!" Shuichi yelled at the top of his lungs. As he yelled, he noticed the guy driving the black car next to him turn and stare. Shuichi's voice was so deafening in the cramped van that Hiro covered his ears.

After Shuichi hung up, he realized that everyone was staring at him. "Ah, sorry, was that too loud?"

The black car in the next lane swung violently toward them.

"Well, that was dangerous," Shuichi said. "Sakano, be careful! Watch the road!" Everyone stared at Shuichi reproachfully.

No sooner had Shuichi spoken, than their van was rammed from behind. The car in front of them had stopped, so Sakano was about to brake, when K suddenly kicked his foot aside and pushed the accelerator to the floor.

"Wow, Americans *do* have long legs," Hiro said, impressed.

K proceeded to shoot the tires out of the car that had sidled up to them. "It's all over if you stop!" K yelled to Sakano. "Drive, drive, drive!"

"Roger!" Sakano shrieked, his white knuckles gripping the wheel. He narrowly dodged the cars trying to block their route.

K reloaded and swiftly rendered the cars chasing them inoperable.

Shuichi watched all of this numbly, as if it was just another action movie on the big screen. "Where's the camera?" he said, suddenly convinced they were on some new variety show.

It's a trick, he thought. After it was over, someone would come out, holding up a sign, and ask them how it had felt to be in a car chase. Shuichi would answer that he was so scared that his lover's face flashed before his eyes.

"I knew it would turn out like this. We're named Bad Luck after all," Suguru whispered to himself.

"Yup, Shuichi always has been unpredictable," Hiro said, his smile twitching.

Shuichi woke up from his daydream. *This really is happening.* Shuichi was getting the impression that everyone was pissed at him because he had somehow caused of all this chaos.

The car screeched to a halt. The sudden stop slammed Shuichi forward into the front seat.

"Damn, they caught us," K said, eyeing the wall of cars that swarmed around him.

Sakano got out of the car and started speaking to the other drivers. "I'm terribly sorry, but would you mind moving your cars?" He walked around, knocking on each window, but there was no response. After a few minutes, he gave up and came back to the car.

K leaned the upper half of his body out of the car and aimed his rifle. "Clear a path out, or I'll open fire!"

But there were no signs of movement. In the cars, young drivers grinned at each other like they were playing some sort of game.

"How naïve! They think I won't really shoot them," K said, switching his gun to fully automatic mode. He fired into the air. Spent shells clinked as they scattered across the asphalt.

The sound of gunfire was so loud that Shuichi covered his ears. "You're just making things worse!"

"They're warning shots," K replied cheerfully, changing the empty magazine. As K started firing again, Shuichi buried his head in his arms.

"Everything with him turns into a war! Go home, black ships! Fight on, Edo government! Seal the country again!" Shuichi shouted.

K grinned manically. "Ha ha ha! What delusions! You're the one who started this war!"

"Don't blame me!" Shuichi cried, but he saw Hiro and Suguru were both nodding in agreement.

Sakano spoke in a voice filled with despair, "I never thought Shuichi would tell them where we were."

"Maybe we should let the president know we'll be a little late," Shuichi said. He pulled his phone out of his pocket but froze when he saw that he had a voicemail. The color drained out of his face as he listened to the message.

"We've been marked," he said, his shoulders slumping as he put the phone away.

While he'd been busy making love to Yuki, his sister had called and desperately tried to warn him that although Bad Luck had been added to the music festival, there was a fan movement to try and prevent it. A description and the van's license plate had been leaked on the Internet.

He had thought everyone was angry with him because he'd been screaming into his phone, but at last he understood.

"Did I just blow our cover?" Shuichi asked.

Everyone nodded emphatically.

"Oh!" A twitch of recognition flashed across Shuichi's face. "You know, I was thinking that this isn't the van we usually use."

Their old van was being used as a decoy, and they were headed to the festival in a rented van. The route they had to take to the festival had also been posted on the website, so they knew there would be a large number of people on the road trying to catch Bad Luck. But they were driving right in the middle of

enemy territory, because they figured the decoy van would draw all the attention. No one had anticipated that Shuichi would shout loud enough to blow the whole plan. After all, few people on Earth possessed a voice capable of carrying through the sides of two cars as they sped down a highway.

"We're quite sure that the same person who spread the rumors about Bad Luck breaking up on the Internet is the one who organized all of this," Sakano explained. "We knew it had to be someone who could come and go freely at N-G Pro, so we began spreading the news in spurts around the office, trying to find the source of the leak."

"But yesterday, Ryuichi heard about you playing in the concert and shouted the news at the top of his lungs," Suguru added. "So everyone in the building knew. He killed our plan."

K nodded. "Shuichi and Ryuichi are two peas in a pod."

"We are?" Shuichi smiled. "That's the nicest thing anyone's ever said to me."

"How can you be so happy at a time like this?" Sakano cried.

"That's exactly why they're alike," Suguru said with resignation.

"It's that damn weird 'net game!" K cocked his rifle. K was referring to a new game where a treasure or target would be selected on the Internet and a large number of people would race to be the first to catch it. "These drivers think that's what they're doing."

None of them had attempted to get out of their cars. They had no intention of actually capturing or doing any harm to Bad Luck.

"But at this rate, we'll never get to the concert in time," K snarled, his gun cocked like an action movie hero. They were trapped in a sea of cars and the police were nowhere to be seen. The only chance they had of getting to the festival was to take matters into their own hands. "Don't you worry. I'm your manager, and I'll never let you down. I'll get these bastards!"

"It's one thing to mess up the bad guys," Hiro said. "But most of these people are just trying to get to work."

"But how do we tell the difference?" Suguru asked.

K's blue eyes flashed. "Exactly, Suguru!" He leapt out of the car, rifle in hand.

Hiro spun around. "K, don't shoot anybody!"

K grinned down at him. "Hiroshi. You've got a motorcycle license, right?"

"Yeah."

K leapt out between the parked cars and blocked the path of a motorcycle that was weaving its way through the lanes. He "convinced" the rider to loan him the bike by tapping the nozzle of his gun against the rider's chest.

"Hiro, Shuichi, hop on."

Hiro leapt aboard, and Shuichi moved to get on behind.

K stopped him. "Shuichi, take this." He held out a small, green pineapple.

"Thanks, I didn't have time to eat breakfast!" he said, before he looked down at the gift. His smile dissolved. It was a grenade. "Um . . ."

"Pull the pin, count to three, then throw it."

"Wow . . . uh, thanks . . . but . . ." Shuichi trailed off.

Hiro asked, "This means we're going alone?"

K nodded. "They're coming after you two. I'll cover you, so you can make your escape. The rest of us will catch up with you later."

"But . . ." Shuichi felt uneasy.

Suguru leaned out of the window. "They're only after you and Hiro. Sorry, but I don't want to get mixed up in your issues."

Shuichi's survival instincts kicked in. "Okay, I get it. We can do this, you'll see." Shuichi turned and held tightly onto Hiro. "Go, Hiroshi, go!"

"Right!" And with one last look back at the others, he revved the throttle. The bike slipped easily through the barricade, and the cars at the front took off after them. K promptly shot their tires out.

"The rest is up to you, Hiro!" he called.

Sakano and Suguru watched the American's rampage from inside the car.

The producer wept bitterly. "I'm so sorry. We've gotten you all mixed up in this craziness. Oh! Whatever will become of us?!"

"Never mind that. I've learned something important," Suguru replied, looking revitalized and totally at ease. "I'm following Shuichi now. I mean, I understand why someone would want to sabotage him—it's because he has real talent. I think I see something special in him."

Sakano sniffed. "Thank you so much! Tohma's blood really does run through your veins! Such insight! Such pluck! I shall follow you!" Sakano flung his arms around Suguru's waist.

Suguru looked down at him, smiling indulgently. "People like Shuichi and Ryuichi can blow through superficial appearances to grasp the true nature of things. I feel like I can do something really great if I stick with people like them."

The young man gazed far into the distance, well beyond the barricade, into the horizon. "Of course, first, we gotta get out of here."

Hiro sped toward the festival. A single black car followed close behind them, having somehow slipped through K's defense. Shuichi clutched at Hiro's jacket.

"What did we do to deserve this?" Shuichi wailed. *Why do we have to take part in a high-speed car chase down the freeway just to get to a concert?* "Can't you go faster?"

"We're already going too fast!"

"Screw it! We're gonna get to that festival or die trying!"

Shuichi pulled the pin from his grenade, and tossed it over his shoulder. It bounced on the hard concrete, rolled, and exploded just in front of the black car, sending a cloud of smoke into the air. They heard the squeal of breaks, but no ensuing crash.

The explosion must have made the car stop, because after the smoke cleared, no one came after them. If nothing else bad happened, they would be able to make it to the festival just in the nick of time.

"We're gonna kick some ass today!" Hiro yelled, elated.

"Yeah, I can feel it. Adrenaline's rushing through my veins!" Shuichi laughed as Hiro's long hair swept back against his face.

The freeway was so clear, it looked like it belonged to just the two of them, a runway designed to send them speeding to success. In reality, the mountain of wrecked cars behind them and the general uproar unleashed by their manager had been mistaken for an act of terrorism. The police had closed the road to traffic. But luckily, the chaos was behind them, completely forgotten, so the two drove on intently toward their destination.

"Shuichi," Hiro yelled over the wind.

"What?"

"My mom's coming to see us today."

"Really?"

"I had a talk with her. You don't need to worry about her anymore. But don't think about that when you're singing. Don't try to make her approve of us. Just relax and sing the way you want to, the way you have all along. Whatever happens, happens. Wherever you go, I'll follow."

"What?" Shuichi cried, unable to hear Hiro over the wind. "We're too ego, while hollow?"

Hiro didn't bother answering that. Shuichi peeked at Hiro's face in the mirror and saw a beautiful, pure smile.

"In front of you!" Shuichi tightened his grip around Hiro's waist. "Look out!"

They were approaching a construction vehicle. To keep roadwork from blocking the flow of traffic, the vehicle had a bridge built on top of it. Construction workers were laboring under this bridge.

"No way!"

As the bike approached, the workers panicked. The highway had been sealed to traffic due to suspected terrorist activity, so they had not posted a lookout.

"Hiro! Brake!"

"Too late!"

The engine roared as the bike climbed onto the vehicle's bridge. The bridge acted as a jump, launching the motorcycle high up into the air. The blue sky spread out before them, and Shuichi and Hiro flew away.

The Fly to the Next Century music festival had been set up on a normally vacant lot. The land had once been a residential neighborhood, but it had been cleared for development during the economic boom and had been bought and sold several times, the price always rising and falling. But when the economy went bust, suddenly nobody wanted it.

The festival promoters had built a circular stage on the empty land, and surrounding this intricate castle was a kind of village made out of dozens of little tents. Countless lights studded the steel framework of the stage, making it visible from miles away, and the open grounds in front of the castle were large enough to hold over a hundred thousand spectators.

The gates had yet to open, and the line to get in wrapped around the grounds several times. The concertgoers were so pumped that the bands that were doing sound checks inside could feel their excitement.

Ask was currently warming up.

"Sounding good," Tohma said, standing just off stage, watching with a satisfied expression. He was at the festival in two capacities: as the president of N-G Pro and the keyboardist for Nittle Grasper. While he waited for his own sound check, he worried about the band that had yet to arrive.

"They're late," he murmured, glancing at his watch.

The decoy car, the one Bad Luck normally traveled in, had already arrived. The grounds were right next to the freeway, so the band shouldn't have been far behind.

"The roads are supposed to be clear."

"Hey! Is that about Shuichi?" Ryuichi asked, tugging Tohma's sleeve and pointing at the TV.

On the screen was an aerial view of the traffic jam, broadcast live from a helicopter covering the music festival. A section of the highway had been sealed off from motorists, and the announcer was relating unconfirmed reports of gunfire and claims that Bad Luck was stuck somewhere in the middle.

"Shuichi can't come?" Ryuichi cried, hugging his stuffed bunny.

"Don't worry. K will get them here, whatever it takes. We have to—"

"What's that?" someone said, pointing to the sky.

"Look out! Run!"

Something that was part-machine and part-flailing-human-limbs flew through the air. The onlookers let out ghastly, frightened screams.

"What on Earth are they doing?" Tohma murmured.

It was Hiro and Shuichi on the motorcycle. They descended, heading straight for the tents. Shuichi let out a piercing shriek. They landed with a thunderous crash, right in the middle of a tent.

Tohma and Ryuichi ran down from the stage. By the time they got to the tent, it had collapsed, and Shuichi and Hiro were climbing out of the wreckage. Although they had flown off the highway hundreds of feet into the air, the tent had broken their landing. They were completely unharmed.

"Dude, that was amazing!" Hiro said.

"Like in a movie!" Shuichi laughed.

They grinned and gave each other high-fives.

Ryuichi ran toward them. "Shuichi!"

"Ryuichi! Tohma!" Shuichi said happily.

"Where'd you come from? Was that a magic trick?" Ryuichi grabbed Shuichi's hands, and they started dancing around like children. "Ever since Tohma said you were gonna be in the concert, my heart's been beating so fast, I couldn't get any sleep!"

"I didn't know I was going to be here, or else I would've been too excited to sleep too!"

"My heart's beating more than yours! Feel!" Ryuichi bared his chest and pulled Shuichi's ear against it.

"Wow! Even Ryuichi's heartbeat is cool!" Shuichi murmured.

As the two idiots carried on, their personalities totally in synch, Taki came off the stage feeling refreshed. But his temporary euphoria ended when he saw Shuichi cavorting with Ryuichi.

"How the hell did they . . . ?" *The news reporter had claimed Bad Luck was trapped in the freeway barricade. How did those bastards . . . ?* He ground his teeth in frustration as his band mates joined him.

"Dude! You gotta hear this!" they said excitedly.

"I'm in no mood for stupid stories."

Ken and Ma looked at each other and continued hesitantly.

"It's just, they say our tent was just knocked down by a flying motorcycle."

"What?" Taki glared at them. "So?"

"So they asked us to share one with Bad Luck, since we're from the same agency and all."

Taki glared. "That's it? That's the big deal?"

Ask's manager led them into Bad Luck's tent. A hastily made card with "Ask" written on it had been posted on the flap.

"We'll take care of the equipment," Ken said. "You wait here."

"You've got to sing later, so you'd better rest up," Ma added.

Ken and Ma left the tent quickly so that they wouldn't have to explain to Taki that it was Shuichi who had destroyed their tent.

"Heh heh heh!" Taki's shoulders shook with laughter once he was alone. "The God of music is smiling down on me today."

He saw some bottles of spring water on the table. A sickening light flashed in his eyes. Carefully, he removed the lid from one of them, poured a small amount of water out, and replaced it with an entire bottle of Tabasco sauce.

"Drink this and spend the rest of the show on the crapper!" he cried, shaking the first bottle, then moving onto the other bottles. Just as soon as the last of the water bottles was stained a garish red, K walked into the tent to perform a safety inspection.

"Hello," Taki greeted him heartily. "I hear you had some trouble on the way."

"Yes. But no pathetic little scheme can stop me! Mwah ha ha ha!"

He continued to guffaw as he inspected the tent. Suddenly, he noticed the spiked water bottles. They were clearly labeled spring water, but the contents were a deep, dark red.

Taki tried to distract K with more conversation. "You're very confident," he said. "But is managing Bad Luck worth risking your life?"

"They've got so much talent, I begged to manage them. I feel sorry for the bastard trying to bring them down, whoever he is. He can try as hard as he wants to, but he'll never have even a fraction of their talent. What he's doing is pathetic, don't you think?"

Taki said nothing, although on the inside he was screaming, *Quit fawning over that lame bunch of losers!*

K strode to the table, looking an awful lot like John Wayne. He picked one of the bottles up and examined it thoughtfully.

"Anyone can have talent," he continued. "But people like Shuichi, people with a true gift, do what they do out of love. They look for nothing in return. They don't try to make people love them more. They just follow their hearts."

Taki bit his lip. *He's not just some wacky foreigner. He's the brilliant manager who got Americans to buy Ryuichi's music in record numbers. He knows everything!*

"Isn't there a Japanese saying?" K asked. "The stupider the child, the cuter he is? I love that kind of guy. So do angels, and so do fans."

With a triumphant smile, K tore open the bottle and started drinking.

"Ah, wait that's . . ." Taki was so surprised by K's action that he nearly let the cat out of the bag.

"Waaah! That's hot!" K gasped for air. He had downed the entire spiked water in one gulp, and his face turned bright red.

K and the others had arrived only a little late, thanks to the efforts of the Japanese police force. The patrol cars that had responded to Sakano's call not only rounded up the young drivers, but also gave the rest of Bad Luck's team an escort to the festival. They had been treated like innocent victims of the Internet plot, even though K had fired his gun.

Sakano, worn out, wailed the moment he saw Tohma. "Oh, Boss!"

"Glad you made it, Sakano." Tohma smiled calmly.

"I am *so* sorry, we tried everything to prevent this from happening. Oh, it was horrible! I thought I'd never live to see you again!" He clung to Tohma, sobbing.

Suguru got out of the car, looking tired.

"You okay there, Suguru?" Hiro asked, smiling. "Did all that make you regret joining this band?"

"I risked my life to get here," the boy replied with a cocky grin. "So let's make this the best show in the history of rock and roll."

"Your words give us courage, sir," Shuichi joked, applauding as if he'd just heard a speech from the prime minister.

"No, really," Suguru said. "I learned something. Wherever you go, Shuichi, I'll follow."

"Then let's see how far we can fly!" Shuichi said, serious now. "Grab hold, we're taking off!"

"How beautiful!" Sakano wept. "Rain has fallen and washed things clean. The ground is fertile again! Flowers bloom anew! We've overcome all obstacles, and Bad Luck has reunited!"

Tohma patted him on the back. "All right, enough melodrama for one day. There's work to be done. The gates'll open any minute, and Bad Luck still needs a sound check."

After the sound check, the members of Bad Luck went to relax in the tent that they now shared with Ask.

"Ah, that felt good!" Shuichi said. "I've never sung on a stage that big! How many people do you think there'll be in the audience, Hiro? A thousand? Five thousand?"

"A hundred thousand."

Shuichi's eyes went wide. "Dude! All of them are here to listen to us play!"

"Bad Luck wasn't even added to the roster until yesterday," Suguru said. "The tickets sold out weeks ago. Everyone's here to see Nittle Grasper."

"You know logic doesn't work on Shuichi," Hiro said. "Especially on a day like today. Anyway, all we gotta do is make all of Nittle Grasper's fans into *our* fans."

"Right!"

Hiro and Suguru grinned at each other.

"Ah, how exquisite! At last the band is unified, the new age of Bad Luck has dawned!" Sakano reached an emotional peak, then collapsed in a fit of coughing.

K's throat was burning, but he reached for a second bottle.

The members of Bad Luck felt energetic and cheerful, but farther back in the tent, a pair of malicious eyes watched their every move.

Track Six:
The Angel's Smile

Yuki had been on a roll when his fingers suddenly stopped flying across the keyboard. He glanced at his watch. It was five minutes before the start of that live concert Shuichi had begged him to watch.

Yuki had hung up the phone and returned to his work as soon as Shuichi had started to yell, but now he saved his progress and left the computer alone. He took off his reading glasses, went to the kitchen, and put on some coffee.

He refused to use instant coffee. Yuki reveled in the deep scent and bitter taste of gourmet blends. No matter how busy he was, he would take the time to grind whole beans and brew fresh coffee.

He poured boiling water over the grounds, and he looked longingly at the brown liquid as it seeped through the filter. When it was ready, he took his first sip and felt his head clear, the effects of his all-nighter immediately banished. Hot cup in hand, he made to return to his study. He walked right past the TV, and sat down in front of his computer.

Just a little bit more, he thought, and his fingers began firing at the keys faster than a machine gun.

Fly to the Next Century started with an opening ceremony that was more elaborate than usual. Fireworks exploded in the sky, their bright sparks flashing on the giant screens placed at both ends of the stage. The crowd went wild with excitement. Afterward, Bad Luck returned to their tent. Now all they had to do was keep their energy up while they waited for their turn.

But just a few minutes later, the tent was ominously quiet. Everyone was sound asleep—Shuichi, Hiro, Suguru, Sakano, and even K, all snored away.

But K was only half-asleep, and a short while later, he woke when he sensed movement. He looked reflexively at the clock. Fifteen minutes had passed. He realized that everyone was sleeping, and grabbed his gun.

"Is this . . . sleeping gas? The enemy is nigh!"

"Enemy schmenemy," Suguru responded, rubbing his eyes. "We're all just tired."

"Yeah, so much happened this morning," Shuichi said. He yawned, stretched, and turned to his partner. "Hey, Hiro, wake up."

"Shuichi." Hiro opened his eyes and froze, sitting absolutely still. "Tell me I'm still sleeping."

"Why?"

"My guitar. It's missing."

"Aw, man, you always gotta joke about that stuff." Shuichi laughed. "We said we'd be serious, just for today . . ." His words trailed off, and he stared, slack-jawed.

Everyone followed his gaze. There was nothing but an empty space where Hiro's guitar should have been.

"Nooo!" Shuichi shrieked, sending everyone in the tent into a panic.

"So my eyes weren't playing tricks on me," Hiro said. "They got us at last."

"This is no time for being calm!" Shuichi howled, shaking Hiro's limp shoulders. "We're on after the band that's after this one!"

Sakano rushed to pull Shuichi off of Hiro. "I'm sure it's just been misplaced!"

"Oh! Oh, yeah!" Shuichi dropped to all fours and started sniffing around like a police dog. "Misplaced!"

Ignoring Shuichi, Hiro started to leave the tent.

"Do you know where it could be?" Sakano asked.

"Nah, just going to get my backup," Hiro turned, smiling lightly.

"Huh?" Sakano was so caught up in worry that he had trouble understanding.

"Good idea," Suguru nodded. "Instead of wearing yourself out looking for it, just get the other one."

"Eh? Eh?" Shuichi asked, still sniffing around.

Their manager said, "Whoever is doing this is trying to keep Bad Luck off the stage, but we won't let him!" K believed the missing guitar to be the work of the same individual who had leaked the rumors of their breakup and trapped them on the freeway.

Blood drained from Sakano's face. "But how? Why?" He fainted. The shock was just too much for him.

"We can't seem to make it more than an hour without trouble," Suguru sighed.

Hiro and K were in agreement: the best course of action was to pretend nothing had happened and calmly deal with the situation. The only way to defeat this particular enemy was to ignore them.

But Shuichi felt differently. "Don't give up! My nose will find it!" he said, sniffing dramatically. Having found nothing inside the tent, he decided to broaden his search to the outside.

"Never mind, Shuichi." Hiro tried to calm him down so that he wouldn't wear himself out before the show.

"What are you smiling about?" Shuichi asked, getting even more agitated. "That guitar's part of the band! It's been with us since we started! Remember, we promised we'd take it on stage with Nittle Grasper someday!" Shuichi's eyes filled with tears, but Hiro kept smiling.

"But I used to play a different one before it. There's no reason I have to play the missing one. Instruments are just tools."

In truth, Hiro agreed with Shuichi. He had been using that guitar for so long, it had become an extension of his own body. But when he considered the enemy's goals, there was nothing else to do but play the backup guitar.

Both the breakup rumors and this latest incident had centered on Hiro, but he suspected that they were roundabout attempts to attack his best friend. The enemy was trying to steal music from *Shuichi,* not from Bad Luck.

"I told you," Hiro said, bracing Shuichi by the shoulders. "As long as I can play with you, there's nothing else I need. Remember?"

Shuichi was speechless.

The members of Ask came in just as Hiro left the tent.

"Fighting?" Taki asked, snorting.

But Shuichi failed to even notice him. "I'm gonna find it! We'll see who's laughing then!" he yelled after Hiro and ran out of the tent.

Although Shuichi's attitude irked Taki, the situation was progressing exactly according to plan. Taki felt so proud of himself that he couldn't hide his evil grin.

Shuichi started searching through the backstage garbage cans. *Maybe it's just a prankster who ditched it in here.* He also checked all the empty equipment boxes and anywhere that seemed large enough to fit a guitar.

"Somewhere nobody would think to look . . ."

It was dark and creepy where Shuichi searched. As he looked around, he thought he saw someone following him. At first, he wondered if it was just his mind playing tricks on him, but every time Shuichi stopped, the shadow following him stopped. When he ran, the shadow moved to catch up.

I'm too busy for this! Don't bug me now! I've got a million things to do! He wanted to shout at whoever it was, but instead, he made as if to run, but stopped and twisted around suddenly.

"Who's there?"

The person froze, poised on one foot, about to step forward. He wobbled back and forth.

"R-Ryuichi?" Shuichi said, relieved. "What are you doing here?"

"Me? What are *you* doing?" Ryuichi asked with great interest, clutching the stuffed bunny under his arm. It seemed he had followed Shuichi out of sheer curiosity.

"I'm looking for something," Shuichi explained.

"I'll help!"

"Really? Thanks!"

Shuichi was about to start explaining what had happened to Hiro's guitar, but he stopped himself.

I can't tell him! I can't make the man I admire the most help me with something as stupid as this! Stop thinking and go find the thing!

"Actually," Shuichi said, "don't worry about it." He turned back around, peeping into the garbage cans and muttering to himself, "It wouldn't fit in here. But where else would nobody look?"

Ryuichi sucked his thumb while he watched Shuichi hunt. After a few minutes, Ryuichi's face lit up with an idea, and he announced it with great confidence: "I know, Shuichi! I know a good place!"

He grabbed Shuichi's shirt and dragged him along.

"Where are we going, Ryuichi? I don't have much time!"

"I know where nobody goes!"

Ryuichi quickly led him out of the backstage area. They emerged in the stage's makeshift lobby, filled with vending machines, port-o-potties, and booths that sold CDs, calendars, and other merchandise. Other than a few staff, scurrying about, the place was deserted. Just a few minutes earlier, there had been so many people it was hard to squeeze through, but now the audience was back in front of the stage listening to the concert.

Shuichi and the others had napped for the fifteen minutes just after the concert began. During that time, many late arrivals had poured in and the staff had been very busy rushing around, so no one would have noticed anything unusual. Sakano and K believed that the thief was somehow involved with N-G Pro or the concert, so the odds of the guitar being hidden here were pretty good.

"Good idea, Ryuichi!" *You may act like a kid, but you sure know what you're doing!*

"You're It!" Ryuichi slapped Shuichi on the back and abruptly ran away.

"Huh? What . . . ?" Shuichi was baffled, but Ryuichi was already out of sight. "Oh well. Gotta find that guitar."

Putting Ryuichi out of his mind, he began checking the makeshift lobby, starting as far away from the entrance as possible, where it looked deserted. Just as he began peeking in the garbage cans, someone suddenly embraced him from behind.

"Eek!" For a second, he thought whoever was after Bad Luck had finally decided to attack him.

"I've been looking all over for you, Shuichi," a voice whispered into his ear. A chill ran down Shuichi's spine. He recognized that voice. Yuki's brother pressed up against Shuichi's back.

"T-Tatsuha?" He was glad it wasn't the thief, but this was almost as bad.

"You lied to me. You said you weren't playing. You pretended to be depressed, and got me to cheer you up. But it was your plan all along to keep Ryuichi all to yourself!"

"No! I wasn't lying! It's very complicated. Look, I . . ." Shuichi tried to explain, while

Tatsuha, still holding him from behind, softly pawed at his chest. "Let go! I don't have time for this!"

"Tell me where Ryuichi is! If you don't, I'll have to take out my frustrations on you." His hot breath coursed over the back of Shuichi's neck. "*Physically*, if you know what I mean."

Faced with this threat, Shuichi squealed like a pig. He pointed in the direction that Ryuichi had run and cried, "He went that way just a second ago!"

"You aren't lying again, are you, Shu-Shu?" Tatsuha playfully bit Shuichi's ear.

"Really! He was running. Hurry, or you'll never catch up!"

"Oh! Why didn't you say so?" He tossed Shuichi aside and ran off in a frenzy. "I'll find you, wherever you're hiding! Today's the day I'll finally make you mine! Wait for me, Ryuichi!"

Flung off balance, Shuichi bounced off a port-o-potty and landed in a heap on the ground. "I don't have time for this!" As his ear pressed against the ground, he heard a strange sound coming from inside the toilet.

"Aw, was someone in there? Sorry!" he said, lifting himself up and bowing his head to the port-o-potty. "I wasn't trying to hurry you up. Please, take your time."

But then Shuichi noticed the color of the occupancy indicator. It was green. There was no one inside. *But I just heard a noise.*

"Something inside here moved when I bumped into it . . . !"

Shuichi flung open the door, and lo and behold, there was Hiro's guitar. His thoughts jumbled together like a kaleidoscope. He leapt onto the toilet seat, grabbed the guitar, and rubbed it gently against his cheek.

"What a relief! Trapped in a place like this, even *my* nose couldn't have found you! Now you can help us make our music heard!"

Just as Shuichi stepped down off the toilet, guitar in hand, the door slammed shut in his face.

"Eh?" He pushed on it, but it wouldn't budge. "What the . . . ? Hey, is somebody out there?

Is that you, Tatsuha? You couldn't find Ryuichi 'cause you stuck around to bully me too long?"

There was a loud rattling sound, the sound of a chain being wrapped around the port-o-potty.

"Whoa, hey, what are you doing?!" The clinking stopped, and he heard the sound of a lock clicking in place. "All right, Tatsuha! I promise I'll make sure you get to meet him later. So, please! I beg you! Let me out! I'm up next!"

"I know. That's exactly why I'm leaving you here," a sinister voice replied from outside the door. It wasn't Tatsuha. "I had only hoped to throw you off. I can't believe you actually showed up here!" The arrogant voice sounded a little familiar to Shuichi, but he was in such a state of panic that he couldn't place it.

"Who the hell are you?" Shuichi screamed at the top of his lungs. "Why are you doing this to me?"

There was no answer.

"Hey! Are you listening? Who are you?"

He kicked the door over and over again, shaking the port-o-potty and rattling the chain.

On the other side of the door, Taki stood in disguise, wearing dark sunglasses and a hat pulled down over his head.

"Who am I?" Taki said, stunned. Everything had gone far better than he had ever hoped it would, and he should have been enjoying his enemy's total defeat, but he was suddenly overcome with the feeling that he had lost.

"You mean, you don't even remember my voice? Am I that insignificant?" Taki was crushed. He couldn't forget Shuichi's voice even if he tried. The song Shuichi had sung when he opened for Ask still echoed in his ears. The resonance of his voice truly rivaled the legendary Ryuichi Sakuma.

It wasn't that Taki hated Shuichi. Spreading the rumors about Hiro and hiding his guitar, never aiming directly for Shuichi—he did all those things because he didn't want to admit what he now realized was true. He was jealous of Shuichi's voice. No, it was even more than that. Taki was *afraid* of Shuichi's voice, the powerful voice of a boy, an idiotic, gleeful boy, who could mesmerize any crowd.

"To hell with it," he said, his voice choked up. He ripped off his hat and sunglasses and threw them in the garbage. The arrogant gleam had returned to his eyes.

"You'll *never* set foot on that stage. The audience will love *my* music instead." Taki turned on his heel, and vanished backstage.

Bad Luck's tent was in total chaos. They had to be on stage right away, but Shuichi was missing. Ask's performance had already begun. According to the program, Bad Luck should have gone before Ask, but N-G Pro had delayed their performance as long as possible. This was their last chance. Nittle Grasper was next, and there wasn't a single band in Japan that could play after them.

"You have exactly one second to find him!" K poked his gun into a security guard's chest. "Or else this magnum's gonna spit fire!"

"Impossible!" the guard replied.

K had inspected the backstage area from top to bottom and found no trace of Shuichi. If he'd left the area, whether of his own free will or under duress, that was the guard's responsibility.

"Impossible? This is your *job!* If you can't find one boy, then you better look for a new career! If anything happens to Shuichi, I'll use these!"

He showed his cufflinks to the guard, who didn't take him very seriously. "This is no time for jokes."

"These may be pretty, but they're my little high-powered detonators. They can make an explosion that'll erase everything within a one-mile radius."

The guard stumbled away, promising to find Shuichi.

K smacked his forehead. "I should've bugged him! I've failed. I knew he was the real target!"

"Don't blame yourself," Hiro said. He had already tuned his backup guitar. The mixer levels would have to be adjusted once they hit the stage, since the concert was already underway.

"Bad Luck, please go to standby," a staff member said, poking his head in the door.

"Right away!" Sakano cried reflexively, waking up from a nap. "All right everyone, let's stay calm and do our best. It's the first concert in a while, so I'm sure you're all looking forward . . ." Sakano finally noticed that there weren't enough people in the room. "Where's Shuichi?"

"He's missing," Hiro said calmly. "He went looking for my guitar and never came back."

"Missing . . ." Sakano reeled back, about to faint again. Suguru caught him.

"Get yourself together, Producer!"

"Yeah. Shuichi would never miss a stage appearance." Hiro flashed his flawless smile, but Sakano was too worried to see it.

"What are we going to do?! All that we went through to get here! Where could he be? Oh! He wasn't kidnapped or something, was he?" Sakano looked ready to collapse again, just as Tohma strode in.

"Has anyone seen Ryuichi?" he asked.

"President," Sakano said. "I'm sorry, but Shuichi has gone missing! We have to cancel the appearance. Bad Luck is finished! I've failed. There is nothing for me to do but atone for this by taking my own life!"

K flipped the gun and held it out to Sakano, but then pistol-whipped him, knocking him out.

"There's only one thing to be done." K stepped over Sakano and started to leave the tent.

"What might that be?" Tohma asked calmly. Even in the midst of this chaos, he was able to keep his composure.

"We're on next. We're going to the wings."

"Without your singer?" Tohma asked.

K arched an eyebrow. "Shuichi will come. As long as he comes before Ask's last song, we can make it work."

Sakano moaned, slowly regaining consciousness. He looked dazed.

Hiro and Suguru nodded in full agreement. Tohma seemed convinced. If he were in the same situation and couldn't find Ryuichi in time, he would probably say the same thing.

Sakano crawled across the floor toward Tohma. "It's too late! We have to withdraw! We can say Shuichi has diarrhea and try to get out of it . . ." Blood trickled out of the gash on his forehead.

"Sakano." Tohma glared down at him. "A professional musician performs for his waiting audience no matter what condition he's in. Do you believe your client unable to handle even that minimal level of commitment?"

"No! They're passionate about their music. I truly believe in them!"

"Exactly. And I left them in your care because *I* believed in *you.*"

"Boss!" Sakano was so overcome with emotion that blood gushed out of his wound.

"I'm looking forward to a great show," Tohma said, sending them off with a smile.

The lights were off and everything was dark when Hiro and Suguru walked onto the stage. Suguru stood in front of his keyboard, ready to go. Hiro walked behind his mic stand. But the center mic stood all alone, the lead spot empty.

An explosive noise reverberated through every fiber of their bodies as their intro began and countless spotlights switched on, blinding them. The audience roared at the flood of sound and light. Anticipation, desire, admiration, and good will erupted from the crowd. Everyone in the audience loved music—their souls belonged to music—and music was what they wanted right now. They wanted rhythm and melody, skill and sparkle, and a voice that could shake them to their very cores.

Hiro and Suguru felt the pressure of the audience's desire.

"Where *is* Shuichi?" Suguru whispered.

When the intro was finished, Hiro looked around the audience searching for Shuichi's face. They started playing the first song of their set.

As they played, the crowd began to notice Shuichi's absence. A whisper ran through the audience, starting near the stage and flowing backward like a wave, gaining strength as it spread.

Bad Luck had no singer. And something else was missing. Their excitement cooling, the audience began to grumble.

Up on the stage, Suguru was playing his keyboard, like always.

"Come on, Shuichi. We're waiting for you!" whispered Hiro. There was no guitar in his hands; instead he held a microphone.

"Hey, everyone, can you do Bad Luck a favor?"

Shortly before Hiro and Suguru went on stage, Shuichi was still in trouble. The door was locked tightly, and no matter how he kicked or punched or threw himself against it, it wouldn't open.

"Dammit! There's nothing else to do!" Shuichi wrapped his arms around Hiro's guitar and squatted down. "I'm in a tight spot . . . literally! Ha ha ha!" His laugh sounded hollow.

He told himself to stop wasting time joking and think of a way to get out, but nothing came to mind. He'd tried shouting and kicking the door, making a lot of noise, but no one had come to find him. *Thanks a lot, Ryuichi. Nobody comes here, indeed.*

"I'm supposed to be on stage with Nittle Grasper! Hiro's mother is here! Today is so important!"

Everything Hiro and he had worked for had led them to this point. Sure, they would probably have another chance to perform live, but today's concert was a once-in-a-lifetime opportunity. They had only one chance to play before the audience that had gathered here, one chance to turn them all into Bad Luck fans.

Shuichi tightened his grip on the guitar.

"And I called Yuki! I begged him to watch the broadcast. I don't really think he'll bother, but if he does, he'll be so pissed that I wasted his valuable time again. He'll be furious! He's the kind of guy who only watches when something like this happens!"

Shuichi began tearing out his hair.

"Crap!" He shouted. "Oh! Ha ha ha. I can't do anything *but* crap in a toilet!"

Shuichi knew that the only one to blame for his predicament was himself. Hiro could have just used the backup guitar. If he'd only listened to the others, if he hadn't made such a big deal about the little details, this would never have happened.

If Shuichi's music was taken from him, he could never lead a normal life. If Yuki was taken from him, he couldn't live at all. That's why he wanted to get Hiro's guitar back.

He couldn't let anyone get away with doing something so horrible to Hiro. Shuichi had wanted to prove that Bad Luck would not give up without a fight. No force on Earth could take music away from them.

"But oh! La la la! Now I'm all alone, and the situation is shitty!" Shuichi droned, depressed. Then something wormed its way into the back of his mind.

"What's that?"

Trying to pinpoint it, Shuichi's ears perked up. *What's going on? The audience is cheering?*

"No way!"

There was no mistaking that intro. It was Bad Luck's first single, their opening number.

"They're doing it without me!"

But he couldn't hear the guitar. What happened to using the backup guitar? Shuichi tilted his head.

"Get real!" came a voice from the audience.

Shuichi agreed. *Yeah, what are you doing out there without a singer? Anyone in his right mind would complain.*

"Where's Shuichi?" another voice asked.

Sorry! In the toilet. But I really don't wanna be here.

"Refund!" a third voice said angrily.

Hey, hey. I'm here! I'm here!

"Boring!"

Something in Shuichi's mind snapped.

"I'm more bored than you! I came here to sing! Let me sing!"

"Sing, Shuichi!" the audience shouted in unison as if they had heard him.

"Huh?" *Wait. They all said that together, all one-hundred thousand of them . . . if they all started* booing at once, I'd never be able to make out any words.

Why demand answers now? Shuichi heard a voice whisper inside his mind.

"Is that you, Yuki?" he asked.

You got this far just on your own passion . . .

The memory of Yuki gave him courage. Shuichi made a decision.

The power of love can move the earth.

"You try to keep me from singing, but that just makes me want to sing louder!"

Matching the music he could hear playing in the distance, Shuichi began to sing. He sang as loud as he could, trying to make the audience hear, trying to make his voice reach Hiro on stage. He sang, and his voice burst out of him, as light as the wind, but as molten-hot as the sun. His voice soared over the audience, across the arches on the circular stage, and reached hundreds of feet to the tents on the opposite side.

Shuichi was trapped on the left side of the stage, while Ryuichi was hiding in a port-o-potty on the right.

"Shuichi is singing!" Ryuichi said to himself. He leapt out of the toilet and ran in Shuichi's direction.

"Ryuichi!" Tatsuha called out as Nittle Grasper's singer passed the entrance.

Hiding his true motives behind a kindly smile, Tatsuha came running up to him. "I've found you at last!"

"Got me. I guess I'm It." Ryuichi, embarrassed, tried to hide behind his stuffed bunny.

Struggling to contain himself at this display of adorableness, Tatsuha quickly asked, "Aren't you playing soon? Are you lost? Can I walk you to the stage?"

"I gotta find Shuichi," Ryuichi whispered, an intense light flashing in his eyes.

The atmosphere of the concert started slowly changing. A few customers had gone to the restroom and heard something strange. They quickly whispered about it to their companions.

"Shuichi is singing!"

The rumor that Shuichi's voice was coming from the least likely of places slowly spread through the crowd. Trying to hear, more and more people grew quiet. Silence spread from the back row. A hundred thousand people acted as one, straining to hear Shuichi's voice.

"Hiro, you were right." Up on stage, Suguru winked, and Hiro smiled back.

"He can't stand disappointing fans."

Hiro's plan to wind up the audience and make them call for Shuichi had worked. The sound from the speakers was slowly lowering, and in its place was Shuichi's echoing voice.

"Impossible!" Taki cried from backstage, where he had been watching what he thought would be Bad Luck's final hour.

Ryuichi entered from the main entrance lobby. He walked toward the stage, followed by Shuichi's voice. The hundred thousand fans broke their silence, but not to cheer. Instead, they expressed surprise with one big, "Huh?"

Shuichi's voice was coming from a port-o-potty that had been propped on a cart.

Yuki, watching the concert on TV, was so shocked that he accidentally sprayed his coffee all over the screen. "What the hell is he doing?"

He reached out his hand for the remote control, ready to turn the TV off, but he froze when he saw his brother's face on the screen.

Tatsuha and a security guard—the same one that K had threatened at gunpoint—were pushing the port-o-potty cart.

Following Ryuichi's lead, Tatsuha had found the toilet Shuichi was locked in, and called the guard. But they didn't have the tools to break the hefty padlock and open the door, so they decided to bring him to the stage, toilet and all.

They dragged the port-o-potty slowly toward the platform. The stunned audience parted to let them through. Suddenly, someone came bolting out from the wings of the stage. As he ran, his long blond ponytail swung behind him. He stopped a few meters away from the toilet and pulled out a gun.

"Good job!" K cried, pulling back the hammer and aiming at the target, squinting his blue eyes. He pulled the trigger. The chains flew apart, and the toilet door sprang open.

Shuichi emerged from inside, clutching Hiro's guitar.

A wave of excitement spread through the audience, followed by whistling and a standing ovation. The crowd thought this stunt was part of the show.

"I found you, Shuichi!" Ryuichi called.

"Ryuichi?" Before Shuichi could figure out what had happened, Ryuichi jumped into his arms.

"I thought you were It, and I was hiding all this time. Sorry!" While Shuichi had been looking for the guitar, Ryuichi had been under the impression they were playing hide and seek.

Shuichi looked around nervously. His eyes found Hiro and Suguru standing on stage. Hiro gave him a thumbs up.

"Go up there and sing!" K said, handing him a mic. Shuichi broke into a run.

Suguru's fingers danced across the keys. Hiro grabbed his guitar and improvised a riff. Then, Shuichi began to sing.

A hundred thousand people fell in love with Bad Luck as they watched the energetic performance and heard Shuichi's passionate vocals. After Shuichi was found, the concert truly became the greatest event of the century. Shuichi sang with a pure, childlike love, a love so strong that it reached even the most distant and uninterested viewers, watching far away on their televisions.

Even Yuki couldn't help but smile. "Idiot." He sat down to watch the rest of the show.

When the last song finished, and Shuichi had let go of the mic, he shouted something that got lost in the deafening applause.

"I did it, Yuki!" Shuichi threw his head back and shouted again. "I did it!"

Epilogue

They were eating a late breakfast in the dining room of the Nakano household.

Yuji flashed a carefree smile. "Happy now, Hiroshi? You get to stay in the band with Shuichi, and now Mom's on board."

"Is that really a good thing?" Hiro sighed, glancing toward the living room. His mother sat there, reading a pamphlet about Bad Luck, looking happier than he'd ever seen her before.

"You're starting to work on your new CD? Think you'll break a million this time?" she asked excitedly. She was reading the 'zine put out by

Bad Luck's fan club. She had already bought fifty copies of their first single and distributed them to all her relatives and neighbors. What his mother had felt watching that concert, Hiro could only speculate, but she had done a complete reversal. She now trusted and believed in her son's dreams.

Hiro looked off into space, smiled faintly, and whispered, "What do parents think of their children, really?"

Her attitude had changed so abruptly that he had no idea how to feel.

"You're acting spoiled again." Yuji laughed.

"Yeah, I know. I don't really want that much out of life."

Yuji ruffled his hair. "All you need is to play music with Shuichi."

Hiro could only nod.

"Yuki, what'd you think of the concert?" Shuichi asked excitedly.

Yuki had finished work for the day and was cleaning up his desk, when Shuichi's arms suddenly wrapped around him.

"You watched it, right? Right? Were we cool? Did you fall in love with me all over again?"

Yuki grunted. "Quiet. You're bothering me." Yuki scratched his head and lay down on the sofa. "I've been up for two days straight," he complained.

"Sorry." Shuichi suddenly deflated. As he sat down gingerly beside Yuki, his cell phone rang.

The ringtone was an unfamiliar melody, so Yuki turned to stare at Shuichi.

"I'll hang up soon," Shuichi promised.

Shuichi grabbed the phone and moved to the opposite corner of the room. He didn't want to bother Yuki, but since he got to see the older man so rarely, he couldn't bear to have Yuki out of his sight.

"Ah, Maiko. Thanks for trying to reach me. But I got it too late," he said, keeping his voice low. Yuki watched him. "Sorry, sorry, it's all my fault. Oh, yeah, we're doing really well, very romantic. Everything's great. Okay, see you then."

He hung up and trotted back to Yuki's side.

"You changed the ringtone," Yuki said.

"Oh, yeah, I did. Got it off the promo site for Bad Luck's new song. Nobody else has it yet. That was the first time in the world it's ever rung!"

"I don't see what all the fuss is about," Yuki said flatly

Shuichi felt dejected. He was very happy that Yuki had noticed the change in melody, but he would have preferred Yuki to be glad for him. It would be nice if Yuki wanted to change his own phone to match. It would be something a couple would do. *It was supposed to be enough for me to be in love, but here I go again, wanting more. I'm so selfish. I can never change.*

Watching Shuichi droop, Yuki said, "There's nothing in your head but music." The words were curt, but the tone was light.

Shuichi's heartbeat quickened at the warm look Yuki gave him.

"And all that craziness yesterday," Yuki said, standing up. "You singing in the toilet. I guess it turned out well, though."

"Yuki!" Bliss made Shuichi's eyes moisten. "You watched?"

"Without music, your head would be an empty shell," Yuki said. "Don't get too carried away."

"Yuki! You *did* watch! You really did!" He couldn't hold back any longer, and jumped all over his boyfriend, sobbing. "Thank you! If it hadn't been for you, I'd—"

"Don't cry! You've got a very loud voice!" Yuki snapped irritably. But he didn't try to pry Shuichi off.

Shuichi had closed his eyes in anticipation of a kiss, but Yuki just sat back down on the sofa.

He cuddled close to the older man, holding him for a long time. "Yuki?"

Yuki was already fast asleep, breathing softly. Shuichi peered closely at him, trying to see if he was faking again.

"Well, he did say he hadn't slept in two days." An idea popped into Shuichi's head. *He probably won't wake up.* Shuichi brushed Yuki's hair back, looking at his lover's beautiful, pale face. He was a demon sometimes, but always an angel while he slept.

Shuichi wrapped his arms around his angel and kissed him without any hesitation.

TOKYOPOP SHOP

WWW.TOKYOPOP.COM/SHOP

HOT NEWS!
Check out the TOKYOPOP SHOP! The world's best collection of manga in English is now available online in one place!

BIZENGHAST POSTER

PRINCESS AI POSTCARDS

I Luv Halloween Glow-in-the-Dark STICKERS!

I LUV HALLOWEEN BUTTONS & STICKERS

- **LOOK FOR SPECIAL OFFERS**
- **PRE-ORDER UPCOMING RELEASES**
- **COMPLETE YOUR COLLECTIONS**

LIFE
BY KEIKO SUENOBU

Ordinary high school teenagers...
Except that they're not.

© Keiko Suenobu

READ THE ENTIRE FIRST CHAPTER ONLINE FOR FREE:

Ayumu struggles with her studies, and the all-important high school entrance exams are approaching. Fortunately, she has help from her best bud Shii-chan, who is at the top of the class. But when the test results come back, the friends are surprised: Ayumu surpasses Shii-chan's scores and gets into the school of her choice—without Shii-chan! Losing her friend is so painful for Ayumu that she starts cutting herself to ease her sorrow. Finally, Ayumu seeks comfort in a new friend, Manami. But will Manami prove to be the friend that Ayumu truly needs? Or will Ayumu continue down a dark path?

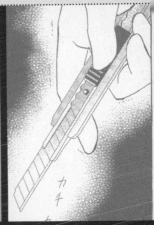

LIFE Volume 1
Keiko Suenobu

It's about real teenagers...

It's about real high school...

It's about real life.

Dear Diary,
I'm starting to feel

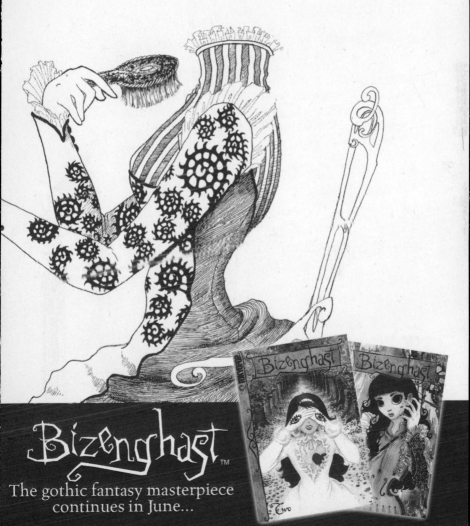

TOKYOPOP PRESENTS

For Believers...

Scrapped Princess:
A Tale of Destiny

By Ichiro Sakaki
A dark prophecy reveals that the queen will give birth to a daughter who will usher in the Apocalypse. But despite all attempts to destroy the baby, the myth of the "Scrapped Princess" lingers on...

THE INSPIRATION FOR THE HIT ANIME AND MANGA SERIES!

For Thinkers...

Kino no Tabi:
Book One of The Beautiful World

By Keiichi Sigsawa
Kino roams the world on the back of Hermes, her unusual motorcycle, in a journey filled with happiness and pain, decadence and violence, and magic and loss.

THE SENSATIONAL BESTSELLER IN JAPAN HAS FINALLY ARRIVED!

THIS FALL, TOKYOPOP CREATES A FRESH, NEW CHAPTER IN TEEN NOVELS...

For Adventurers...

Witches' Forest:
The Adventures of Duan Surk

By Mishio Fukazawa

Duan Surk is a 16-year-old Level 2 fighter who embarks on the quest of a lifetime—battling mythical creatures and outwitting evil sorceresses, all in an impossible rescue mission in the spooky Witches' Forest!

BASED ON THE FAMOUS
***FORTUNE QUEST* WORLD**

For Dreamers...

Magic Moon

By Wolfgang and Heike Hohlbein

Kim enters the enigmatic realm of Magic Moon, where he battles unthinkable monsters and fantastical creatures—in order to unravel the secret that keeps his sister locked in a coma.

THE WORLDWIDE BESTSELLING FANTASY
***THRILLOGY* ARRIVES IN THE U.S.!**